ASSESSING MY VALUE:

Thoughts from a Trailblazer in the Real Estate Industry

Marcus Hill

I0541742

First Printing

ISBN Paperback 979-8-9877149-1-4
ISBN Hardcover 979-8-9877149-0-1
ISBN E-Book 979-8-9877149-2-8

Printed in the United States of America
www.askmarcushill.com

DEDICATION

To my late grandmother, Earnestine Lockhart, this book is for you. I hope I have been living a life you have been proud to see.

This book is also dedicated to my family, friends, and those who have found their passion for a career.

FOREWORD

Phillip Thompson, Certified Residential Appraiser

I was prompted to go into the appraisal business by my dad. I grew up watching him appraise property, and once I finished college, I started working with him and developed a passion for the profession.

Once I entered the profession, I saw that it included a low percentage of people of color. So, when I received my license in 2003, I was just as focused as my dad was on bringing in more of them. Since then, I have trained six people of color, with three obtaining their appraisal licenses.

One of the notable qualities I saw in Marcus when he came to work for me was his passion for the profession from the start. I initially had him file paperwork while also explaining the business to him. Some of the terminology and procedures were difficult for him; however, he was eager to learn everything he could, and he never became discouraged. Marcus was a big help to me and with his passion and determination, he was able to earn his appraisal license and open his own business within a two-year period.

My proudest moment was seeing Marcus become successful in this profession and help bring in other people of color on a national level. Marcus' ability to bring the appraisal profession to people on a national level is a vision I wish I could have carried out. Marcus is using his passion and platform in a major way.

I hope Marcus's book inspires readers. Through him, they will see that with hard work and dedication, anyone can achieve their goals regardless of their circumstances.

PREFACE

In 2007, I became a double unicorn in the home appraisal industry.

Before my 27th birthday that year, I received my appraiser's license in an industry in which even today, 1.3% percent of African Americans are represented, according to the first quarter of 2019 Appraisal Institute's U.S. Valuation Profession Fact Sheet, which is the largest professional association for real estate appraisers. The majority of these practitioners (50.7 percent) range in age from 51 to 65. However, I started in the appraisal industry fresh out of college at the age of 24. The percentage of appraisers 25 or under at that time, according to that fact sheet, was only 0.9 percent.

Not only was I an anomaly in the industry, but I was a successful anomaly. After receiving my license, I left the company at which I apprenticed and put out my own shingle as an appraiser. As I stepped outside the box to build trust with local banks, mortgage companies, and real estate agents, I branched out further by also going to work as a mortgage originator, credit-repair expert, and owner/landlord of multiple properties. (These are my opinions and do not represent any other entity).

I'd come a long way from being raised by a single mother in a tough Little Rock, Arkansas neighborhood — a neighborhood that had been featured in the infamous 1994 Home Box Office documentary "Gang War: Bangin' in Little Rock." A neighborhood in which it was common to hear shootings going on, witness crimes being committed, and see acquaintances, friends, and sometimes even relatives led away in handcuffs.

I enjoyed several key benefits that kept me from following the paths of those I saw around me. One, I had a good, God-fearing mother who kept me on the right path. Two, I had a grandfather to whom I was close and who did the same. Three, I was part of a close-knit church community that, from the pastor on down, included positive male mentors who had an impact on my life. And four, there was always something inside me.

Something that made me determined not to bend to peer pressure and become another negative Black male statistic.

So, I bloomed where I was planted. I went to historic Central High School, where I made a name for myself playing football and making the grades.

As a teen, my main goal was to attend and graduate from college. I reached that goal, graduating from the University of Arkansas at Fayetteville no less. (Growing up in Arkansas, you want to go to the No. 1 college in the state - especially kids who grow up as Razorback fans.) I was the first of my mom's children to go to college and earn a degree.

I couldn't have imagined the other firsts and milestones that were to come.

PART ONE:
MY JOURNEY

INTRODUCTION

A Message from my 92-Year-Old Grandfather

My grandson, Marcus Hill, has always been attentive to what came next in his life and what he needed to do to be successful. He doesn't play around with anything; he attends to business. He's always busy, always striving.

Marcus has always been Christ-like, adhering at all times to what would be best for himself and those around him. As he grew up, my hopes for his future included the hope that he would aspire to whatever would be beneficial to him and his livelihood. That hope was realized. He strove for education and strove to be the kind of young man anyone would want to be around.

Although he grew up in a tough urban environment, Marcus never allowed other people to influence him when it came to the destiny he planned for himself. I had no worries that his surroundings would affect him. Sometimes, your environment is something of which you wouldn't want to be an example. You want to pursue what would be best for you, and not be influenced by anyone or anything else around you. That's how Marcus was.

The most memorable piece of advice I gave Marcus was during his days of playing high school football. I told him to make sure to always do those things that would bring honor to his teammates and to be obedient to his coach. As time went on, I saw that he would be a man whom people would consider an example and want to follow.

When he told me he was going to start his own company, I was surprised and excited. I looked for him to be what he'd have to be as he went into learning how to be the best in his field.

I remember, when I was working as a plumbing inspector, the times I took Marcus to my office in North Little Rock. He didn't realize at the time that I was one of the only Black plumbing inspectors for the city. He has experienced the same thing I did, except in real estate. What he wanted to do was work in his field without being worried about his color or his surroundings. He did those things that worked for him.

I was proudest to see Marcus' story told in the High-Profile section of the Arkansas Democrat-Gazette in 2022. He stood out as one of the most successful, innovative young men in the community - one who had followed the examples his grandfather had set for him. Dreams I had for myself were realized with Marcus.

I attended Philander Smith College for two years. But I was so proud to see him head to the University of Arkansas at Fayetteville and go all the way - not giving up and determined to be his very best.

When Marcus built his own company and then left Little Rock to work for the government, I was proud of him for being unafraid to step out there.

The most important thing to know about Marcus is that he is happy to share his expertise with others. He has conducted workshops for young Black people about the appraisal system; when these students are ready to go into that industry, they already know it's an industry in which they are very much in the minority, but they won't have to worry about that. They will be equipped with the knowledge my grandson taught them.

And, having attended Marcus' workshops for the undeserved communities, I hope his book will teach people all they need to know about real estate and appraisals, as well as how to overcome adversity.

God has been looking over Marcus all his life. And he knows that God has had His hand on him.

We find in Scripture the parable of the servants that were made rulers over many things because they were faithful over a few things. Marcus is proof that there isn't anything too hard for

God — if you are destined to be an outstanding individual, God will see to it that you become one.

- Alvin E. Lockhart, Retired Plumbing Inspector

Chapter 1

Laying the Groundwork

College was a whole other story for me. My high school football career was successful enough that I went to the University of Arkansas as a Razorback football player under then-coach Houston Nutt. This was my first time on my own and that was scary. I'd never been away from my mother or my grandparents, who lived right around the corner from my mom and whose home I would head to every morning to have breakfast before going to school.

Honestly, I just had a particular mindset coming out of high school. I knew I was going to graduate from college but being on my own was quite an eye-opening experience.

Some people think that being a student-athlete is living the life of Riley... "Oh, they just play football or whatever." No, it is a job within itself to go to class, write papers, participate in group projects, and at the same time attend practice and work out. In college, there's nobody pushing you or staring you down expectantly when it comes to your academics. No one saying, "You'd better do this/that or else." The onus is strictly on you to do the work. You have to be self-motivated, and self-driven. If you don't do the work, you get an F. The attitude of the professors is, "Here's the introduction to adult life."

So whatever people's attitude toward college may be, it's definitely an introduction to independent living. I recommend it because as an 18-year-old, unless your parents or mentors warn you — "OK, this is how you need to start living" — you don't really get it. You don't have to go to class. You don't have to write the paper. You don't have to create the project. But there are consequences if you don't.

Coming from that "Bangin' in Little Rock' environment and entering college I thought, "Wow, this is crazy. All these people are going to class on their own, trying to do something positive." To me, that was amazing. But it was even more amazing to be a student-athlete. In addition to going to class, you have to learn a playbook, go to practice, and work out. The combination of those responsibilities was a bit overwhelming. Student-athletes go through a lot that people just don't see. For instance, going running in the morning, then having to make an 8 a.m. class. It can be an overwhelming experience. But it also helps prepare you for the discomforts and hardships life will bring later.

On the whole, I loved the experience of being part of the Razorback football team and meeting people from various parts of the country.

I was at the UA from 2000 to 2005. Unfortunately, I ended up getting hurt in the middle of my eligibility period - a shoulder injury. I could have gone into rehab and kept playing, but there was also the very real risk of re-injuring my shoulder and making it even worse. I concluded that "This is probably God telling me, 'Hey, this, this is enough; I've got something else for you.'".

However, that was quite an adjustment for me because I had been playing football since I was about 7 or 8. To do something for that long and then find that you can't do it anymore can be jarring. Had I hoped to go to the pros? I believe every college athlete has that aspiration. But my injury played a pivotal part in the course of my life.

The good thing is that I never lost sight of the real reason I was in college. Yes, I loved playing sports; it was great. But I wanted to graduate. That was my biggest thing. I was an athlete, but I didn't really engage in typical, off-the-field "athlete" activity because I knew I had a goal. I had come from a hard upbringing. And I was trying to stay out of trouble, trying to do the right thing. I always felt the need to properly represent and honor my family, even while away from them. There were a number of things Coach Nutt said that resonated with me, like, "Do what's right when nobody's looking." I feel that as a college student away from your family, you've got to do just that. (Many families have no idea what their young people are getting into while away at college.) Now I'm not saying I didn't enjoy a party or two! I just didn't go as far as some of my classmates did. I didn't get into anything I couldn't walk away from. I knew my limits.

Again, college provided me with a wonderful opportunity to train for having the mindset and ability to work with people from all walks of life. If you graduate from high school and immediately go to work, you don't really have the time to develop your communication skills. Nowadays, you've got to have the mindset to do your job correctly, from working with your manager to working with the public. If you didn't go to college, you have to learn it through on-the-job training. College gives you the opportunity to gain skills that you need — the ability to work effectively and responsibly, work with all types of people, and especially develop a spirit of integrity — knowing that if you don't do the right thing, or do that right thing correctly, you're going to get the boot. College helps you build all the skills that are going to help you ease into the real world. It's like a "pre-real-world" setting.

Again, I was self-motivated because my goal was to graduate. I was excited about attending class, reading textbooks, writing papers, and taking tests. I think about the movie, "Higher Learning." Even though it has this crazy plot, I could relate to the setting of young people in college. And then, as a young man growing up in church, I was inspired by fellow members who left and went to college. I told myself, "You can do that too."

At UA, I met many good people with whom I'm still connected today. College is also where I entered fraternity life — Kappa Alpha Psi Fraternity Inc. When you're part of a football team, you, and your teammates bond for sure because everybody has to do their part. But where college really paid off for me was in becoming part of my fraternity, which presented another environment that represents achievement in every field of human endeavor and stresses the importance of doing the right thing. I took that to heart. I was impressed by this group of students who were all about community service. It really did something for me to be a part of an organization of people doing positive things, whereas I'd once seen so many people doing negative things.

I repeat my admission that I was attracted to the partying aspect of fraternity life — that was good too; I mean, it's a part of it. But when I first noticed this group of cool, confident men, that resonated with me. They represented even more than what I'd initially envisioned for myself, because once I became a part of Kappa Alpha Psi, I revved up my mindset and was even more about achievement, positivity, and about community. Those were the characteristics within the fraternity that I would take to heart. It was definitely a process going through that, but I think that process helps you with life too because not everything in life is going to be perfect. You're going to have some stumbling blocks; you've just got to know how to pick yourself up.

So, it was an amazing experience to not only be a student-athlete but also be a part of a fraternity as well. I had the best of both worlds, and it was amazing to be at the state's top college. (Coach Houston Nutt had attended high school at my alma mater, so there was that Central High School connection as well.)

Those life lessons I learned as a college student had a huge impact on me. I learned how to work with people and how to be part of a group/team with a goal and a mission. But I also learned to be on my own and set and reach goals. I knew I had to read the material. I knew I had to write those papers. I knew I had to study for this or that test. I knew I had to do these things because if I didn't, I wouldn't achieve my goal. Unfortunately, I knew students who had to drop out because they lacked the needed determination. Some became involved in activities that led them astray. But that's how I wanted to separate myself from my neighborhood where I'd been around so many people who were not doing positive things.

I did a double major – in criminal justice and sociology. The reason I chose criminal justice is because I'd been around so much crime growing up. I wanted to understand the criminal mindset as well as the social side of that criminology. I saw the two as going together.

I wanted to go to law school. I have a cousin who became a lawyer and works with the University of Arkansas at Little Rock Bowen School of Law. I looked at his life like, "Wow." I looked up to him. He inspired me to learn about the law and go down his path, so in my senior year of college, I started to prepare myself to go to law school. In college, I was building a mindset, building integrity, and building a work ethic. I told myself, "Hey, you achieved a goal. What do you want for yourself now?" I wanted to make money, I wanted to be on my own time, I wanted to impact my community in a positive way, and I wanted to be able to support a family if I had the opportunity to marry and start one.

So, I was about to move back to Little Rock, go to Bowen School of Law, and go down the same path my successful cousin had followed.

But then, things changed.

Chapter 2

A New Direction

There's a particular family, the Thompsons, who are members of the church in which I grew up. When home, I would run into Phillip Thompson, who's around my oldest brother's age. I'd see him periodically at church, where his dad taught Sunday School.

During my senior year, Phillip asked me, "What are you going to do now? You're about to graduate I see." I told him about my plan to return to Little Rock and attend law school.

"Hey, you want to come work with me for the summer?" he asked.

I was like, "All right, you gonna pay me? Whatcha doin'?"

Phillip had his own home appraisal company, Elite Appraisals. I'd achieved my college graduation goal and was open to new experiences, so I said "All right, yeah, man. I'd love to see what you're doing."

I didn't know then, at 24, that I would become one of the youngest in America to even begin training as a Real Estate Appraiser. In those days, you had to have a college degree to do so. That was interesting because I didn't know much about real estate. As a kid, we lived in apartments and rented houses. We never owned anything. My mom would eventually own a house, but when I entered the real estate industry, it and all its aspects were foreign, even crazy to me. You see houses and apartments every day, but entering the real estate industry, you're looking at them from a totally different vantage point.

At any rate, I was so open to this opportunity. I wanted to make sure I was doing everything right. I wanted to display a good work ethic.

When I went to work for Phillip, the first thing he had me do was organize his files. After you do an appraisal, you have to keep a work file on it for a certain amount of time. If that deal ever comes into question, the file will show all aspects of it — the exterior and interior of the property, its square footage, and all other notes taken on it. The first thing that I did as an appraiser trainee was organized two years' worth of Phillip's work files.

And the area of Phillip's office in which the work files were located had no air conditioning.

I was like, "OK, you want me to do what? All right. I'll do it; I'm just happy to be here. What do you need done? Boom — I'll do it."

It took me two to three weeks of organizing Phillip's entire two years of work files, putting them in chronological order so they would be easily accessible should they be needed. Despite the discomfort, I kept the same attitude I'd always had — "What do you want me to do? OK, boom, I'll do it." I would come to find out that having this mindset would work in my favor. It pays to be willing to do the dirty work. (There's definitely a different kind of mindset needed to be in real estate, period.)

Years later, Phillip remarked "You know what? I asked you to do that even though that part of the office was hot, and you went in there and knocked it out and didn't complain or anything." This let Phillip know that I was going to be serious when I started working on actual appraisal matters. Having the willingness to do the dirty work paved the way for big things.

Another way Phillip tested me was by sending me to photograph residences. He'd tell me, "Hey, I need a picture of this property." I remember driving to Conway, Arkansas, and my initial thought is, "I've got to drive all the way out to Conway for one picture?". (Making home appraisals start out with having the right photo; you need an accurate image of the property to document its existence.) But again, I was not one to complain about the little stuff.

I took photos for a while, then one day I went with Phillip on an actual inspection. I was crazily surprised because as a real estate appraiser, you have to have a certain eye for things and be able to recognize certain things about a house. That's how I first learned the process - watching Phillip.

So, at age 24, I entered the appraisal industry - and not the typical way. Nowadays, most people start out taking appraisal education courses. Phillip gave me the opportunity to gain experience first, which would help me greatly. By the time I began my coursework, I had already gone on property inspections and was already familiar with some of the appraisal terminology and issues. At the time, I didn't realize I was blazing a trail.

When you go to appraise a home, you typically must have a clipboard, pen, and paper because you're going to have to write out the property description — exterior and interior. Back in the day, you also had a 100-foot measuring stick, but these days they use measuring lasers that can calculate the length of the exterior walls. You also have to have a camera.

Some things I began to learn as I went along on inspections with Phillip:

■ Properties are properties, but their conditions may vary. That really caught my attention. Your average homeowner may never even think about home characteristics beyond whether it's built in a particular style, has visual/curb appeal, is big enough, or has the number of bedrooms and bathrooms desired. Homeowners may not dwell too much on say, the advantages and disadvantages of brick, frame, or stucco exterior walls, or a roof made of asphalt, metal, or clay.

■ As an appraiser you've got to look at a property like you've never looked at it before because you have to accurately explain the characteristics of that property. Learning that was a huge thing for me. I'd lived in a house, but I'd never looked at a house as a real estate appraiser looks at a house. A house that looks like it's about to fall down may have "good bones", whereas a late-model McMansion may have been constructed by builders who cut corners and therefore may be a big, dressed-up mess. People can rehab properties, but sometimes they don't do it in what we in the appraisal business refer to as a "work-man-like manner."

■ There are common issues that will tip an appraiser off that a home has problems, i.e., cracks in the walls indicate a foundation problem. I developed an eye for noting property conditions. I remember during my first inspection of a property seeing settling cracks in the exterior brick and knowing that was a problem that needed to be noted.

■ As I was making my observations, I realized that integrity is key when going into the appraisal business. An appraisal is an impartial and unbiased opinion of a property's market value, which goes back to what I had learned in college — going to class and doing what I needed to do without anyone having to look over my shoulder and make me do the right thing. Integrity in appraising is everything because you are tasked with giving an impartial opinion of a property's value. Other people are going to make lending decisions off your numbers.

There are so many different, equally important factors in the appraisal industry - things you have to get right. Determining the square footage of a property for instance. That's one of the most important factors in each appraisal. The square footage number goes into the appraiser's report and lets homebuyers and lenders know the size of a house. It was amazing to go onto properties and learn how to measure them.

I was struck by the importance of an accurate appraisal, period. As an appraiser, you don't want any inaccuracies in your report. You are responsible for everything in that report. You must be able to explain every single thing in it, especially if litigation over the property ever arises.

The appraisal industry is also powerful in that you, the appraiser, can stop a deal. If you're doing an appraisal that involves a $200,000 contract on a home, but you have determined that said property is really worth only $190,000, everything stops. Your client has to go back to the realtor and renegotiate the value of that contract. The buyer could also bring the difference to the closing table. That's why you have to make sure you know what you're doing. People are making major decisions because of you. That's how important this industry is.

Chapter 3

Birth of a Career

The appraisal industry is one of the only industries in real estate in which you're guaranteed to make money. In America today, if you get a mortgage loan, you're getting a federally-backed mortgage transaction. An appraisal is going to be required because lenders don't want to lend more than what properties are actually worth. People buy and sell every day, appraisals are done every day, and appraisers must be paid. You can deal with one realtor one day, then switch to another one the next if you feel the first realtor is not representing you well. You can go to a bank and get one mortgage interest rate, then go to another bank and get a lower rate. An appraiser who's hired to inspect a home must, according to law, be paid, regardless of what may be in that appraiser's property report.

So, I'm with Phillip for the summer, and I'm seeing all these orders for appraisals coming in — "Another one? Another one? Wow, this is amazing. The bank is going to pay me every time I do an appraisal? Hmmm. If I go to law school, I'm not really guaranteed to make money. But if I learn appraising, I will have created a life for myself." When I started working with Phillip, an appraiser could earn as much as $400 per house (the pay is much higher now).

I knew that this business was going to be my jumpstart to earning good money at a young age and allow me to be in ownership of something. With college, you earn a degree, and nobody can take that degree from you - You did that. It's the same thing in the appraisal business; once you learn the skills you need to know to be able to set the value of a property, nobody can take that away from you.

I came to this realization at the age of 24. Now your average 24-year-old in America is still trying to find himself; he's probably trying to party and have a good time and isn't really taking life seriously yet. But once I witnessed the workings of the appraisal industry, I saw how serious this was and how lucrative it could be.

Another thing I saw at 24 is that if I learned and entered the business, I could be the youngest African American in this industry in the state. I may have been the youngest person ever in America to be learning this particular skill. I got started in the summer of 2005. Based on the aforementioned information from the Appraisal Institute, there are less than 1% of appraisers under the age of 25 in the industry. That was in 2019! Just imagine what those numbers must have been in 2005.

Now Little Rock is not a major city like Dallas, where I lived for 10 years while writing this book. As an appraiser in Little Rock, you may know very well the neighborhoods in which you are appraising homes; you may even find yourself in the neighborhood in which you grew up. (There's no telling how many times I've been to where friends used to live.) You're looking at these properties with a whole different perspective because now you're trying to figure out what they are worth.

The first rule in appraising: Identify the problem. This rule is the same whether the property is being appraised for a purchase, a refinance, or just a determination of market value. Going into the area where I grew up in Little Rock was certainly interesting. I lived on 22nd and Park streets and there's a duplex around the corner. I still remember playing over there as a kid. I actually had an opportunity to appraise that same property when I started my company. I found it interesting and somehow symbolic: I used to live in the area and there I was about to put a value on a property around which I actually played and hung out with friends!

Of course, regardless of neighborhood, you may even know the people whose homes you are appraising. There have been a few times I showed up to do an appraisal and found a friend's family member there. They were like, "Oh! You do appraisals?"

As an appraiser, you have to go into properties not only of various sizes and styles but various conditions. Some may be pristine; unfortunately, some are not the neatest or the cleanest. Many bank-owned properties, for instance, are trashed out. I remember going into one bank-owned property in particular. There's usually a lockbox on the door and a combination code required to enter the home; however, in this particular case, homeless squatters were in the house. When I put in the code and opened the door, there they were! As an appraiser, you've got to be aware that those things are going to happen. Sometimes properties are trashed out so badly, it's not safe to walk around in them. That can't sway you. You've still got to do your best to get the square footage of the house, take pictures and describe the home's condition — while doing whatever you need to do to stay safe, of course.

Then I remember going to appraise a mansion-size home. It took me a long time to measure that big house, but I had to stay there and get it right because the client expected me to do so. I say once again that doing the difficult jobs properly goes back to integrity - doing what's right as an appraiser.

When I was with Phillip and realized appraising was the business I wanted to follow him into, I set my mind to enroll in the courses I'd need to take. Appraisal licenses are state regulated; every state has its own licensing requirements that must be fulfilled. Those requirements include a certain amount of coursework.

I began taking real-estate appraisal courses in 2005. At that time, most of the courses were in-person. In every course I took, I found I was typically the youngest student and the only African American. In passing, I'd wonder, "What's going on here? I never see anybody who looks like me in these courses." That same lack of youth and diversity was going on in every city in America at that time, and today there are still less than 3% of people of color in the industry.

But, although I noted that there was no one who looked like me, I didn't really dwell on it. It was mainly a matter of Phillip telling me "Hey, these are the classes you've got to take," and me thinking "OK, this is what I've got to do."

These courses were quite interesting; they were all two days long, $300-$400 each. You would take a test on the last day; if you passed that test, you got credit for the course. If you didn't pass the test, you'd have to pay again to retake that course. That put a lot of pressure on me. There I was, in these classes sanctioned by the Arkansas Appraiser Licensing and Certification Board, trying to meet licensing requirements. The cost of the courses is, I believe, one reason for the lack of diversity — people are not going to pay to take these courses just on a whim. But, at 24, I didn't have any bills. I was working with Phillip, who was paying me as a trainee. I simply used some of the money I was earning as a trainee to pay my tuition.

These courses were taught in different towns in Arkansas. I would just as likely have to travel to, say, Jonesboro or Russellville to take a course as take one in Little Rock. Again, in every course, I was the youngest and the only African American. My classmates were white men in their 40s or older. I look back and I'm amazed that I even had the mindset to be there. Yes, sometimes it felt like I got the side-eye from those classmates. But I believe they were side-eyes of respect. I surprised myself being in that environment. And again, it helped immensely that I had already gained field experience. Today, most appraisal courses can be taken online.

To prepare for a career in appraising, you've got to learn a lot of material — from math to ethics to appraisal procedures — that's not easy. You have to train your mind to think like a property investigator. You have to learn many terms. You have to learn the inner functions of a property. (People can live in a property for decades and not be familiar with the terms that describe the interior and exterior workings of their home - terms that describe everything from plumbing to electrical.)

Learning business so young gave me confidence. I'd already learned, through my fraternity, how to build confidence within myself. Going through these classes helped me in even more ways.

Then came the day, during my training, that Phillip was involved in an automobile accident in Tennessee. Phillip would travel to various places on business, and he'd taught me how to mind the store in his absence. And I mean he'd taught me everything — how to talk to bank and mortgage company officials as well as appraisal management companies and homeowners — and, of course, how to do appraisals. And, during the week or so that Phillip spent recovering from his injuries, I ran his business. If a bank or appraisal management company needed a correction on an appraisal, for instance, I'd take care of it.

Phillip recovered from his injuries in a hospital in Memphis, so I drove there to check on him. I told him, "Man, I've got you. I know how to run everything." When the average age of an appraiser running his own company is 50 years old in America, I was doing it as a trainee at half that age.

That's when something clicked in me — "You know what? If you get your own license, you can do this yourself. You are confident enough. You have the tools. You have the mindset. You have the integrity."

When Phillip recovered, he returned to the office. Business was good; we didn't miss a beat. I think he really respected me for how I handled things. I'd been taking all the calls, doing all the inspections, handling all the matters with the banks, doing the inspection reports, talking to the agents, and talking to the homeowners. I concluded that this was what God put me here to do. He gave me something that is really tough to get into, but I already had what it took for this particular career. And I was open to Phillip giving me the opportunity.

Chapter 4

The Final Steps

Back in the day, an aspiring appraiser had to put in about 2,000 hours or so apprenticing with an appraisal company. I put in the hours and, once I finished the courses, submitted my credentials to the Arkansas Appraiser Licensing and Certification Board for my license.

To this day I can remember what it was like once I made that submission. The appraisal board sent me a letter with my interview date — once you submitted all your education and experience hours, you had to go through an interview before taking the licensing test. One of the required submissions was a certain number of appraisals done while apprenticing with a company. During the interview, the board would take a few of these appraisals and ask you about details in your reports. I can't stress it enough — you have to know the business because a financial institution is about to loan someone money based on your conclusions as an appraiser. If you don't know what you're doing, the consequences could be dire. Going through the process, I could see why they make it tough. If you don't know how to properly place a value on a property, you can be sued, or potentially go to jail - so many different things can happen to you. You're valuing the biggest asset Americans have - their home! And there I was at a young age, learning how to value a person's wealth.

Anyway, I got my interview date and asked Philip what the process was like. He briefed me.

I feel I benefited not only from Phillip himself but also from Phillip's dad, Mr. Thompson, who was also part of the Arkansas appraisal story. He was the main person who was responsible for the majority of the state's Black appraisers. He's the one who actually gave them, along with his son, the opportunity to get into the Appraisal Industry.

So, I also reached out to Mr. Thompson to ask him about his experiences and find out what the life of an appraiser was like. I also got a lot of feedback from others who had gone through the interview process with the board, others I suspect, who had never seen anybody young, and Black go through the process.

Fast forward to the day of the interview. I woke up that morning with a plan to put on my nicest suit and at least try not to look like I was 19.

That's right, I didn't even look my age! Just imagine me going to inspections and knocking on people's doors looking that age — and I'm about to value their wealth. Knowing what I know now about the appraisal industry, if I were a homeowner about to undergo an appraisal of my property, it would really shock me to see somebody young about to do it, especially somebody who looked like they just graduated from high school. I mean, there you are, about to refinance your home; you're trying to pull say, $20k out of your property, and you see somebody who looks like they're fresh out of high school. You'd have some mixed feelings, and you'd probably have some reservations. I remember I'd always get questions like "So... hey... how long have you been doing this?")

When I got to the interview, I was so nervous. I don't think I have ever been as nervous as I was that day. It was already nerve-racking going to these appraisal courses.; not only that but talking to real estate agents, knowing that they know most of the appraisers are older made it even more worrisome. And then to go before the Arkansas Appraiser Licensing and Certification Board? I was extremely nervous. But I knew that I knew my stuff.

So, I walk through the door and everybody's just looking at me, like, "Can we help you?". Imagine what it was for the appraiser board to see me walking in there saying "My name is Marcus Hill, and I'm here to do my interview so that I can take the appraiser licensing test." That's crazy within itself! There were other people there — all older of course — and I could see them looking at me.

I wait until my turn comes around then go before several gentlemen from the board. They're asking me these questions whose answers I had better know if I were to become a licensed appraiser. At this point, I'm sweating. I know what I was told before I got there: If they don't feel you know your stuff, they're going to deny you; you won't even make it to the licensing exam.

They're asking me questions like, "On this page of your appraisal report, how did you make these adjustments?"

I tell them, "I did it like this," and I break it down for them. Every question they ask me, I answer correctly. I'm on point, telling them exactly what they want to know — how I came up with a property's square footage, why I made this or that adjustment pertaining to a property, how I came up with its adjusted gross value, how I implemented the comparables. They then start to look at me like, "OK, he knows his stuff."

I remember them finally saying, "All right, well I guess we're done here."

I was on Cloud Nine. I had just gone into a setting in which nobody expected me to know as much as I knew at my age. They didn't realize that I'd totally found my passion even though I'd grown up in an environment that did not reveal such a career choice to me. Yes, I was nervous; I was scared. But I knew that I knew my stuff. The interviewers knew they could not deny me. I was approved to take the licensed appraiser's exam.

From there, I went about securing my test date. I knew it would be another nerve-wracking experience, but I could see what would happen once I was issued the license. I saw Phillip getting appraisal orders multiple times a day. I knew that if I had that license in hand, my life was going to change. There were other people who'd worked for Phillip in the past who didn't get things done that quickly. I'm sure Phillip at some point thought, "This guy is 24 years old. He's not about to go out and start a business. He's probably going to be with me until he's about 30, 35." But what Phillip didn't realize was the degree of my passion for the business. He gave me the opportunity to learn the business which gave me the confidence I needed. And I was determined that if I got this license, I would do what I needed to do to prosper. I wanted to live the life I felt I deserved; the life I once didn't feel I could have. Even had I gone to law school, graduated, and passed the bar, I doubt I would have started a company, especially at the age I was.

The appraiser's licensing test was sure enough, particularly challenging. What most people don't know about the industry is that not only are appraisals done for home purchases and refinances; but also needed when banks foreclose on a property. In addition, appraisers are used to value homes when married couples divorce — they typically need an appraisal to split the equity in their home. When people change their mortgage insurance, they need appraisals. Plus, there are tax-related appraisals. I knew if I had this license, I would always find work somewhere.

So, I went to take the exam. I knew that I'd know the answers to many of the questions I'd be presented with, but with a test that important, and with that level of difficulty, you just never know. I knew that just to get to the point of even taking the test was an amazing achievement within itself, whether or not I passed. (There are no statistics on appraisal trainees, but it's a safe bet to say there weren't many African Americans training and testing for such a career fresh out of college at the time. I'd graduated from college in May 2005; I was training with Phillip by that summer, and it was now 2007. So, I'd had no break.

Most appraisers have post office boxes; in appraising, you typically get paid when the deal closes. In an average home sale, the buyer closes on the home within 30 days. So, you're checking your P.O. box every single day because you may have a check coming in — some days you may have as many as seven or eight checks in your box.

I, on the other hand, was looking for a letter from the board to hit my P.O. box, having been told I'd get my test results in the mail in a few weeks. I can still remember going to the box one day and there it was. I took the letter and went back to my car in the parking lot of Phillip's office. Before opening it, I said a prayer and did some reflecting. I thought about all I had gone through, making it into college, then getting into this field about which I'd become so passionate, and learning all the things I'd learned during training.

"You know what," I told myself, "whether you pass or fail, you accomplished something big, something not too many young Black men even experience." To summon the determination to achieve a major goal in an environment where nobody looks like you and nobody's as young as you is no small thing.

"You accomplished so much so quickly," I told myself. "Whatever happens, you should feel proud."

And I did feel proud. I give much credit to my grandfather, who served in the military and was the first Black plumbing inspector in the city of North Little Rock. When I was younger, I wanted to accomplish something too. I didn't know what that was. Then I found myself going through the process of becoming an appraiser, something I never thought I would experience.

And I saw what this career can do. Phillip was traveling everywhere, living the life. I remember thinking, "Wow, I want to live like that someday." I wanted to drive a nice car. I wanted to travel. I wanted to set my own working hours. All the things I wanted coming out of college were the very things the appraisal business would be able to supply if I'd passed that test.

I still remember opening the letter there in the parking lot and seeing that I'd passed.

When you grow up like I did, you have to have a certain mindset of overcoming to keep from following the crowd, to be different, and to prepare yourself for opportunities. So, there were a lot of emotions running through me. I was crying in my car because I knew my life was indeed going to change from that day on. All my hard work was about to pay off. I was about to become one of the youngest African Americans in Arkansas history to be licensed in this industry.

"You know what? I passed my test," I told Phillip. "But you know what else? I think I'm going to try this thing on my own. I think I'm going to start my own company." He'd always pushed me to keep going in this business, so he understood.

And I felt that God was telling me 'Hey, it's your time now."

Chapter 5

Leaving the Launchpad

I was eager to strike out on my own. Reaching out to another church member, I obtained information on how to start a business. It helped that I had people in the community supporting me, including some of the elder members of my church. My grandfather gave me startup cash, a laptop, and software. That gave me even more confidence to just go for it.

Phillip, of course, was also immensely helpful. When I first went to work for him and he asked me to file those papers, he probably needed that task done, but again, I suspect it was a test to see if I was willing to put in the work. He knew as an appraiser, that this is no easy industry to enter or navigate. I think he wanted to check my temperature so to speak, to find out whether I had the mindset to do something this difficult and actually accomplish it. I don't think he realized at first just how motivated, ambitious, and driven I was.

The Ins and Outs of Appraising

Let me explain more about the business of real estate appraising.

The beauty of the industry is that you're not only doing appraisals in case of purchases or refinances. As I pointed out earlier, appraisals are required when banks foreclose on a property when divorcing couples need to figure out how to split their home equity in cases of insurance concerns, and for various tax-related matters.

To you introverts out there: Typically, in this industry, you really don't have to deal with many people. You are going out and doing appraisals. Once you receive an order from a bank or mortgage company, you set an appointment with a realtor or homeowner to visit and inspect the property. Properties also have lock box codes on them so you may not have to see anyone at all.

Home Appraisers Vs. Home Inspectors

Often, people get home appraisers mixed up with home inspectors, but the two jobs differ.

Appraisers and inspectors both do interior and exterior inspections of properties. Typically, you access the home inspector through your realtor but you access the appraisal through your lender.

An appraiser is gathering information about the property to tell the property's quality and condition, two of the main factors that come into play in the appraisal industry. But the appraiser is only going to do an interior-exterior inspection on what he can see of the property. For instance, if the roof looks like it needs to be fixed, he's going to jot that down. If the interior needs drywall repairs or needs to be painted or the floor needs to be redone, he's going to note it. If the kitchen is updated, he's going to note that as well. He's going to consider factors such as these in the final reconciliation of the property value.

The appraiser is also going to measure the property and get its square footage while doing the exterior-interior inspection. (Some appraisals are just "drive-by" appraisals. A company may have a real-estate asset and request that an appraiser does a drive-by of that asset. That means taking a photo and doing an analysis based on an exterior inspection.)

The home inspector is going to go deeper. He's going to go over that property from top to bottom, down to its roots and bones.

Both the appraiser and inspector will indicate whatever repairs are needed. But as the appraiser notes only what he sees, he may not be at the property that long. Based on what he says (depending on the type of loan the buyer is getting), a lender may require repairs to be made before the deal goes through. Again, that shows how much power the appraiser has.

The home inspector's report is going to be sent to the homebuyer, who can use that report as a negotiation tool with the realtor so that any deficiencies the inspector found can be fixed before closing. You can close on a home no matter what a home inspector's report reveals, but if an appraiser notes an area of concern, the lender may not allow closing without that issue being resolved. The main problem an appraiser may list — something that is almost sure to get a red flag before closing — is settlement or foundation issues. Once that's on a report, you may have to get an engineer out to give an OK before closing, just because the appraiser noted it.

From the home inspector, you're going to get a list of issues, and the inspector may or may not put a value on the repairs. But for any repairs that the appraiser lists, he's going to give an estimate of a "cost to cure." That's the other thing about an appraiser; he will determine repairs and repair amounts to fix issues on the property. (When you're an appraiser, you learn all these things you can typically use in personal business dealings as a real estate investor. More about that later.)

Working Through the Downturn

In 2008, 26 and confident that I could make a good life for myself, I opened an S Corporation. And guess what happened that year? The Great Recession and the housing crisis.

But the fact that there exist multiple ways appraisers are utilized was in my favor. Even though I'd stepped into a down economy, I created work for myself.

I was a young, minority appraiser, which was not common in Little Rock, so I knew I would have to make myself known. To do that, I had to think outside the box. Luckily, I learned a lot from my mentor, including thinking outside the box (as well as different types of business deportment).

One of the things I did was attend Chamber of Commerce luncheons. At these events, they offered people opportunities to talk about their businesses. I never shied away from any opportunity to tell people that I was an appraiser.

Then I'd do the unexpected. I remember waking up one morning with a novel idea to bring breakfast to everyone working in the mortgage department of a particular bank. I did this out of the blue, having never worked with that bank before and not knowing a soul in the place.

Before 2008 appraisers typically would have to go to banks, or a vice president or head of a mortgage department, to try to get on their appraisal list. I wasn't the typical person they saw every day. So, I knew I would have to make myself seen. When I presented breakfast to this mortgage department, I said, "Hello, I brought you guys breakfast. I want to pass out a few cards to let you know that I'm here; I'm a licensed appraiser." Wanting to separate myself from other companies that had been in business for years, I told them, "Hey, I will give you the same quality as the appraisers you know. But I will get your appraisal back in a 48-hour turnaround." Back then, the typical turnaround time for appraisals was about a week. (It probably got up to two-three weeks during the summer 2022 housing boom. But a week was typical back then.)

I even put my promise on my business cards — "48-hour turnaround time" — just so they'd remember. I was single, I didn't have any kids and I enjoyed my job, so I was in the position to make good on such a promise - and make clients think twice about walking away from me. If a lender client gets that appraisal back in 48 hours, that client can tell a homebuyer that they'll be able to close quicker than other lenders.

So, this particular bank took a chance on me because I thought outside the box. They gave me a shot and boom! A positive domino effect. I went on to work with banks and multiple mortgage companies.

I continued to attend Chamber of Commerce events. I went to "business after hours" events, at which I'd always see a representative of another bank whose business I wanted. I'd tell him, "Hey, how's it going? I do appraisals; here's my card." (I always tell young people: If you just continue to show up, be consistent, and be confident in your craft, people will give you the chance. And once you do get a chance, you've got to show up. You've got to go above and beyond. That's what I tried to do every single time — think in terms of "Where can I place myself to let people know what I do?")

During this time, appraisal management companies were kind of a big thing. Many banks give their appraisal work to these companies, so a new appraiser would often sign on with one. Appraisal management companies became prevalent after the Dodd-Frank bill was passed in Congress. As explained on the website FindLaw:

The Dodd-Frank Act, also known as the Dodd-Frank Wall Street Reform and Consumer Protection Act, was enacted in 2010. It was a direct response to the financial crisis of 2008 and the resulting government "bailouts" administered by the Federal Reserve under the Troubled Asset Relief Program. The Dodd-Frank Act initiated a broad range of reforms affecting nearly every aspect of the financial system to prevent a repeat of the 2008 crisis and the need for future government bailouts. The Act also sought to establish additional protections for consumers.

That law was a way of encouraging more impartiality in our business. Back in the day, mortgage people could pick their own appraisers and there was a good chance they'd pick people they already had a relationship with — if you know what the sale price of a property is and you got Johnny Appraiser that you've been working with for years and years and years. Well, it was what it was.

Yes, the Great Recession was a trying time. But again, there are multiple reasons people need appraisals. In addition to those I've already mentioned, investors were buying homes. Heirs to a property owned by someone who'd passed away needed to know the value of a home so they could split the proceeds from its sale. People simply wanted to know the general value of their homes for whatever reason. Yes, I was worried at first, but I channeled that worry into thinking outside the box and putting myself out there. That's another beautiful thing about the appraisal industry: even in a downward economy, people are still going to need you.

And it wasn't just homebuyers I worked with. Remember the first rule of appraising I mentioned? It was to identify the problem. Yes, individuals are purchasing properties and need your value assessments. But so do companies. Even if a company is flailing and in danger of going under, its officials still need to value the company's assets to see what those assets are currently worth. That helps those officials make decisions on what to do next.

And I point out again that the appraiser, once hired, will be paid no matter what. I remember having a handful of appraisal jobs at a time with this particular bank. Typically, a bank or mortgage company will send you an order and you will carry it out. But you won't get paid on a deal until 20 to 30 days later when the buyer closes on the house. In this instance, I remember becoming somewhat worried: "Hey, these loans aren't closing because people are losing their jobs." I figured buyers were not going through with the purchases because of financial hardship. But by law, you the appraiser must be paid whether or not those purchases are made. That is power - being in an industry where you receive an order, carry out that order, and get paid whether or not the objective of that order plays out. I saw this while working with my mentor. I was like, "Wow, so you mean to tell me that no matter what, I get paid?" Yes. So, I still did very well amid a national financial crisis.

A sad note - yes, I found myself doing quite a few foreclosure-related appraisals during the rash of foreclosures that occurred during this time. But Arkansas really didn't get hit like California or New York because the median property value ranges in Arkansas cities are not as high as they are in bigger markets. For instance, a bank may foreclose on a $200,000 house in Arkansas compared to a $2 million property in a big city. Still, foreclosure is what it is.

It was definitely interesting to see the trends around the country while everything was tanking. People were losing their jobs and trying to refinance when they found themselves underwater on their mortgages, owing more than their homes were worth. Honestly, many people who had obtained mortgages should never have been allowed to do so. Before the crash, adjustable-rate mortgages had been big; these mortgage holders had a certain payment for about three to five years, then once that period ended, they had to be able to refinance or else their payments would increase substantially. All too many people found that due to job loss, pay cuts, or inability to qualify, they were unable to refinance.

Then there were the mortgages that were subprime in the first place and helped fuel the Great Recession. "Economists cite as the main culprit [in the recession] the collapse of the subprime mortgage market — defaults on high-risk housing loans — which led to a credit crunch in the global banking system and a precipitous drop in bank lending," according to an article at businessinsider.com. "By [the] early to mid-2000s, the residential housing market was booming. Mortgage lenders rushed to approve as many home loans as they could, including to borrowers with less-than-ideal credit."

Throughout that recession, I continued to build my business.

I ran an appraisal company, but I was always looking for ways to utilize my skill set to help people even more. I wanted to learn everything I could about real estate, so in addition to wearing my appraiser hat, I worked as a loan originator on the side with another company. Working largely with potential borrowers in Pine Bluff and Little Rock, I got to see all the ins and outs of what it takes to get someone qualified for a loan. Some days I'd be wearing my home appraisal hat; some days I'd be wearing my mortgage originator hat.

To set myself apart even more, I told the realtors I was working with, "Hey, just send me your people, whether or not their credit is good. If their credit is not good, I will do credit repair for them and let them know exactly what they need to know." This helped me keep a pipeline between the realtors and potential future borrowers. A realtor who knew that a person's credit might not qualify them for a mortgage at the time would send that person to me so that I could work with them, letting them know what they needed to do to qualify for a mortgage in the future. I worked with multiple realtors in the city and never really had to market that business because they already knew me from my work in the appraisal world.

At one point, I was working with seven agents in one office in Pine Bluff, doing group seminars during which I told people about the steps to qualify for a loan. I was able to aid people who thought they would never get into a house because they'd not had access to someone who would show them what they needed to do.

That was a really high time in my life. I was so motivated! I felt I could do anything in real estate. And I expanded my business even more. I started buying single-family homes and rented out these properties, along with doing a little home flipping. As an appraiser who's buying properties, you have quite a bit of power. You already know the value of the property before you get there; you can see what someone paid for the home, as well as what you're about to appraise it for. You know how to estimate repair costs. And you know what you can sell that property for. You know it all. So, I thought, "Why can't I buy and sell properties? Let me learn this business too because I just made this guy $50,000 off the value I declared for this property." For a person who's in real estate, that's power.

Once I started my company, I just wanted to learn it all. I had so much motivation and so much ambition. I felt that I could do anything at this point, having started an appraisal company, one of the most difficult aspects of real estate. Going to real estate school is not that bad. You can do that in a few months. Being a loan originator, same thing; you go through the courses and take the test in the same amount of time. But home appraising? That is not going to be an effortless process. As I've indicated, it's going to take some work. You're going to have to be patient. I understand why they make it difficult. A bank or mortgage company is about to lend money based on what you say. There's so much responsibility and power that comes with the job. As an appraiser, you make a deal stop or make it go.

And you've got to be personable and establish rapport with your clients. I was working with these banks and high-level mortgage companies, but I was able to make every single client feel like I was working with them only.

Truly motivated individuals are usually doing much that you don't see. As I mentioned previously, I promised clients a 48-hour turnaround on appraisals. That meant there were nights when I was up until 11 p.m. or midnight working on reports to get ready for the next day. Sometimes I worked all day. But I was averaging as much as $400-$600 per report. I was working at home, for myself. I was getting appraisal checks, mortgage origination checks, and checks from rental properties, all at the same time. And I was a good steward of my blessings; I never abused the business or did anything out of the norm. I allowed myself only the luxury of travel. I'd work a few weeks, then maybe take a week off and go out of town.

For a long time, nobody knew what I was doing. People would see me around town or see me in the neighborhood measuring a house. But I really just kept to myself. Eventually, my reputation grew.

Now there were times when clients wanted me to do unethical things, trying to take advantage of my youth, my Blackness, and their assumption that I was wet behind the ears. Let me explain. The appraisal report comes blank. You can, as an appraiser, put down whatever information you want. You can give a value to a property that is not really worth that value figure. This is why when studying to become an appraiser, you go through ethics training, which is a very high priority. People would come to me saying, "Hey, I know your fee is $500 but I'll give you 3 to 4 times more if you give me more value on my property."

I had to disappoint them. It wasn't worth it to me. I knew that I had to show the utmost integrity. I was a millennial, a member of a demographic stereotyped as unwilling to work. I was Black. And I was going into people's homes. I knew I had to build and maintain a sterling reputation. An appraisal report is a federal-related transaction on which financial institutions are making lending decisions. When I completed an appraisal, I had to sign that report, which meant that everything in the report was my responsibility. If someone came along, possibly years later, looked at my report, and saw that something didn't add up, I'd be the responsible party. So, it didn't behoove me to do anything unethical.

I also never tried to complete any assignment I was not competent or qualified for. I never did anything that would even appear to be improper. God gave me the desire to do something that few other young people in America were doing. I had an amazing opportunity, and I always wanted to represent myself, and my family well.

Chapter 6

Through My Appraiser's Eyes

As a real estate appraiser who was, well, not your father's appraiser, there were multiple times I would go to banks, mortgage companies, or networking events, hand people my card, and get a look like, "What???". And there were multiple times I'd go to people's houses, knock on their doors and they'd be like, "Hello, can we help you?" I'd tell them, "I'm Marcus Hill. I'm here to do your appraisal." Then everything would change because they knew I was about to value their wealth. And to see the shock on people's faces was priceless. There I was in my mid-20s, looking like I was 19. And there I was knocking on people's doors in Little Rock, where there's a tiny number of African American appraisers. To see someone so young as well as Black was a shocker for many homeowners.

I always just tried to do my job to the best of my ability. What I made sure to do as an appraiser was spend a generous amount of time with each client. I knew they were going to have questions. I knew they would want to know whether I knew what I was doing. I would sometimes stay as long as an extra 20 minutes, answering homeowners' questions. Every time this happened, I could sense that they had been a little uneasy about me. But by the time I left, they had an attitude of, "He's going to a good job because he answered all my questions."

I'm sure I got more questions than other appraisers normally would. I was used to that because when I was going through my courses, I would be asked more questions than others in the class were typically asked. Luckily, I did not experience any blatant racism from those I worked with. And it wasn't just from white homeowners that I got more questions than I felt I would have gotten otherwise. I got them from other people of color in general, and other African Americans in particular. Perhaps with them, it was strictly an age thing; they saw that I was young, and although they may have dealt with appraisers in the past, they'd never seen anyone like me before. I suppose racism could conceivably raise its head in the guise of a challenge to the value placed by an appraiser of color on a white person's home. But my value to a property was only challenged one time out and that too may have just been due to my age.

Overall, I can say I did receive the respect I was due. There's a lot of respect that comes to those who hold that hard-gained appraiser's license.

Appraisin' in Little Rock

I've been all over my native city. In an average month, I did probably 15-20 appraisals a month there. Appraising homes in Little Rock opened my eyes to the real estate goings-on in the older neighborhoods (including my own) as well as newer and reborn ones.

We, appraisers, are utilized to give different types of values to properties - new construction, existing properties, properties that have been rehabbed, and trashed-out properties. These values include an "as-is" value, a "repair" value, or a "subject-to" value.

Subject-to values apply to the reborn neighborhoods (some prefer to use the term "gentrified"). The East End of Little Rock, now known as East Village, is a major example. As an appraiser, I helped to start values in subdivisions in the area, which had been predominantly Black. When someone wants to create infrastructure for a neighborhood development, they have to order a subject-to-appraisal. The bank will have an appraiser give a "subject-to" value in which the appraiser takes the plans and specifics from the architect and bases a value on those plans and specs. The property does not exist yet. But the appraiser will take the plans, specs, and also the square footage for the future property, and produce a value as though it did.

In other words, the appraiser is being asked: "Can you state what this property would be worth if it were already here?" I did multiple appraisals in which I'd start a value standard of a new neighborhood. Once an appraiser puts a value on a potential property, that property becomes a "comparable" for someone else who might want to buy in that neighborhood as it develops.

I remember doing some appraisals in the East End, as well as another predominantly Black area where there was new-construction interest. In an older neighborhood, you may as an appraiser, find no comparables. In that situation, you would do your best to try to find properties that are similar, even though the neighborhood homes are not new construction. You just have to find the best available property in order to produce a value.

I was doing appraisals in west Little Rock, Pine Bluff, North Little Rock, Jacksonville, Conway, and Saline County. But when I got opportunities to do appraisals in the neighborhoods where I grew up, that hit really home. I'd made it to a point in my life where I had the opportunity to put a value on my former stomping grounds. I appraised properties I saw while growing up, looking at these neighborhoods with new eyes. I was like, "Wow, I used to play around the corner from this house. But now here I am, charged with the duty to place a value on it."

Going through appraisal training and learning how to distinguish types of properties and discern their condition — to view a property differently than you would merely be living in it — was a revelation. As a new appraiser, it became my job to know how to describe a property, label its condition, measure it accurately, and pull comparable property sales in the neighborhood. (Just living in a house, you wouldn't think about these things. But again, as an appraiser you have to familiarize yourself with a property to the point that a bank can make a lending decision based on what you've noted about that property). What was really an eye-opener was seeing vacant, boarded-up properties from a different perspective and knowing that even those dwellings have some type of value. It's a perspective we often don't understand about anything property-related: even in the worst neighborhoods, the houses are still worth something. The land is still worth something. You see these houses that were built in the 1950s, '60s, and '70s in a particular neighborhood, and you don't think much about them. But when you go through training as an appraiser and you are charged with producing a value, it makes sense. That property may need to be rehabilitated, but it has value.

I think of a boarded-up house in one of my old neighborhoods; people have doubtless driven past that house and dismissed it as not worth much. To me, it's worth everything, because I know what's going on in the neighborhood. I'd like to help Black people in poor neighborhoods understand that those neighborhoods are worth much if we only knew. (Somebody else knows!) In our community, we don't understand values. We don't understand how a house can be rehabbed and how someone can then profit from that house once it's fixed up. What if we valued our less-thought-of neighborhoods and worked to boost their property values?

A case in point: As I re-explored parts of Little Rock prior to the publication of this book, I saw two new-construction, two-story homes by Dunbar Middle School, the landmark of the Dunbar Historic Neighborhood, one of the older predominantly Black neighborhoods. I've never seen new construction in that particular area. Because I know about property values, I know that certain things in the area are changing for the better. I think about the similar metamorphosis going on in Hanger Hill (now known as the Hanger Hill Historic District) in what was known as the East End. There's a yacht club (!) there now, in what was once a crime-ridden area. If we understand how to really value property — in particular, see what's been dubbed undesirable property through a different lens — we would truly advance economically. Whereas we may see a boarded-up, trashed-out house and decide nobody wants it, an investor says, "That's exactly what I want because I know I can put a little bit of money into this property, then it'll be worth more and I'll make a profit."

One thing I'm planning as I'm writing this book is to find more creative opportunities to share with the youth and adults about things I've discussed here and more. Stay tuned.

Chapter 7

A Date with Fannie Mae

Once I got into appraising, I took it far. I daresay there were few, if any people in America at the time who were running an appraisal company, doing mortgage loans, flipping houses, and owning/managing rental properties at the same time, by themselves in their 20s. I had truly found my passion.

I will be honest: I didn't have a life. I was working a lot. I did try to enjoy myself, but I felt the pressure because I knew I had no colleagues like me. Still, I enjoyed the pressure because I knew that I knew my stuff. And people were willing to give me a shot. "Hey, we know this person is not the typical person to do this, but maybe we should give him a chance. He had the audacity to bring people breakfast. He had the audacity to say, 'Hello, I'm an appraiser. I know that you've never seen anyone like me before, but I'm here. And if you want to give me a shot, I would be a good steward of this opportunity.'"

In the real estate industry, you have to find your niche, that thing that separates you from others. If you can do that, you will have a constant flow of business. If you're the type of person who can articulate well and is always willing to meet people, talk to them, and share with them, you're in luck. Armed with all these things, I put myself out there. And back then, I was so excited to have a business and so excited to be in this great profession. Every single day was an enjoyable one for me. I was doing something I loved to do.

And then, Fannie Mae and I met up.

Just as I'd dreamed of doing, I was working for myself, working when I wanted, and traveling when I wanted. But I'm also like my grandfather, who always had a "challenge yourself" spirit. I told myself, "Hmmm, I've never been in corporate America."

I'd gone from graduating from college to training at an appraisal company to starting my own company, so I'd never had the experience most people have when they finish their postsecondary education, going to work in corporate America. Being where I was, yes I felt comfortable. But having grown up the way I grew up, I had a philosophy: Never feel comfortable. You can always do more. So, I told myself that if I ever got an opportunity to do something on a major corporate scale, I just might leave my comfortable life.

When my mentor introduced that opportunity, I was open to it. It was something I thought was never going to happen: a chance to work with Fannie Mae, a leading source of mortgage financing in the United States, as a valuation analyst.

I thought, "OK, I'll go ahead and apply." I did so through a recruiter company, not thinking I'd get the job. At the time, a minimum of 15 years of appraisal experience was required, and I had fewer than 10. But…I was hired!

It was January 2012, a weird period for me; sometimes the appraisal industry, lucrative as it is, can be up and down. But I had not planned for the possibility of being hired, because I didn't think I was going to get the job. Despite all I was doing in the industry, I didn't think they would even consider me. I was in little ol' Little Rock. This was dealing with the big boys!

I told myself, "Well, this is it. This is what you asked for as far as being open to changing your life, even though you're comfortable working for yourself." Something in me said this is the next thing. This is the next challenge. I prayed about it. And I felt like this was indeed the next thing.

I was told to report to work in a week and three days. I was like, "Okay, this is it."

The job was in Dallas, so I had to move to Dallas. Aside from college, I never lived anywhere else besides Little Rock. I had to tell my family, shut down my company, and figure out what I was going to do with my house.

I didn't know what to expect. Having never worked in corporate America before, I didn't know how to navigate it. I was thinking, "Wow, I'm my own boss. And I am going to put myself in a position where I'm going to have a boss?"

But my spirit continued to tell me, "This is the next thing." I felt I would learn more. I'd be around more experienced appraisers. I think at the time, in this particular department at Fannie Mae they'd never heard of anybody so young coming to join them; I knew my coworkers would be longtime veterans from all over the country. To me, the aspect of learning is huge because it was instilled in me that learning is how you take yourself to the next level. I felt this would be an opportunity for me to get out of my comfort zone; to see if I could still be successful doing something out of my norm and doing it well.

So, I packed my bags and moved to Dallas. I had a friend from college who happened to live near my office, so it was an easy transition. I stayed with my friend for six months while I got my bearings.

My job at Fannie Mae involves properties all over the country. Immediately, I started learning about the different property types in various cities and states. As an appraiser in Little Rock, you're just appraising properties in Arkansas, so you've got certain styles/designs. But at Fannie Mae, I was immediately thrown into a situation where now I was viewing properties all over America, having to learn different markets, having to learn about other property types, and having to learn how to estimate repairs on larger scales. I had to take all my knowledge as an appraiser in Little Rock and apply it on a national scale while learning the corporate lingo.

But being open, thinking outside the box, and having an amazing work ethic helped me immensely, as did all those things I'd learned professionally. Those soft skills, such as working with people, exceeding expectations, having grit, embracing your passion, and knowing that whatever you face, you will eventually figure things out and do well. I was now in an environment where everybody was looking at me wondering "What was it about you that qualified you to be in this position?" What most people at Fannie Mae didn't know is that due to what I'd been through, I had the mindset, smarts, and savvy of someone who had been in this business for years.

Honestly, I'm still in awe to have the opportunity to be in this position and to be able to say that I have worked this particular craft at the highest level. I'd never thought about home features such as clay roofs, basements, mud rooms, accessory dwelling units, or ADUs (guest homes). These are features you generally don't find in Arkansas, the exceptions being the basements found in Little Rock historic homes.

As a Fannie Mae valuation analyst, I began learning many new things. Learning to read all the markets was amazing. You have to know every single market in the country; that's part of the job. And you have to know the different property values according to geography. In the South, for instance, $500,000-$600,000 will get you a home that's at least approaching palatial. You might have a house and land worth a total of $500,000. Well, that's how much the land by itself is in some areas. Some people in big cities in the Northeast and West (think New York and Los Angeles) have never seen a $500,000 house, because the minimum home cost in these areas is anywhere from $800,000 to $1 million. In these cities, a million dollars, let alone $500,000, may get you only a tiny fixer-upper, an outright shack, or a shed.

What you can't put a value on is actually learning all of this. It's priceless knowing all the things you have to know to put values on homes on a national basis. Knowing what impacts the market in a particular place, and what drives the economy there. Also learning the true importance of supply and demand. These are all the things that I had to learn.

Honestly, to be at this level is one of the greatest opportunities I've had in my life. It's something not many people in the appraisal industry get to see because the majority of appraisers work only in their city of residence. They don't get to see the types of properties that lie elsewhere. I've had the opportunity to see just about every type of home design. I've seen and learned just about every market. And I've been at it for 10 years as of this writing. In the appraisal industry, not only can you become licensed in your state of residence, but you can also go beyond the boundaries of your state because you have the knowledge and expertise needed by corporations and other business entities. So, I've had the best of both worlds: being an appraiser working on a local scale, but also being a valuation analyst working nationally. I am probably one of the only people my age and race in the country who has had both opportunities. But it all started with trying to be good at something; having a passion for a particular career and learning everything about it, enough to make me marketable in any kind of valuation position. I had no idea that loving the appraisal industry would take me this far.

My job as a valuation analyst requires no business travel. Everything is done remotely. We have vendors in every state. They do the legwork. We play more of an analytical role. We analyze the reports on the properties and place values on them. The beauty of valuing homes on a national level really brings home the point that according to an understanding we have in the appraisal industry, every property is different. Two properties can be in the same subdivision, and bear the same style, but still not be the same. Each dwelling has its own individual characteristics. I knew by being a part of Fannie Mae, I would learn so much. I was seeing so many other different property styles — Craftsman, Greek Revival, Italianate, Contemporary, Georgian, and Midcentury modern — and increasing my knowledge base.

What I must say is that my experience with the mortgage giant has been a once-in-a-lifetime opportunity. Not only has it been amazing being around other experienced real estate appraisers and valuation analysts from around the US, but it's truly the culture and people at Fannie Mae that make it a wonderful place to come to work every day.

Chapter 8

A New Role: Speaker in the House(s)

During the 18 months before writing this book, I added another role to my career repertoire — public speaker. I share my expertise with various groups at colleges, nonprofits, and other entities.

For 15 years of my career, I didn't really share much about myself with anyone. But one day I found myself in a meeting and saw those Appraisal Institute fact-sheet statistics I shared earlier. I looked around the room and was like, "Does anybody see this?" It was 2020; I believe it was around the time of the murder of George Floyd, a Black man, at the hands of a police officer in Minneapolis and the nationwide protests that resulted.

I thought to myself, "You know what? I need to do more than what I've been doing."

So, I reached out to a few people I knew were associated with schools. I thought maybe I should seek an opportunity to share a bit of my story with the youth, just to see what their response would be. This was the first time I "got the spirit" to share myself. I was excited.

I recall the day a friend of mine was on the phone with someone, and I asked who it was. "Oh, that's my speaker coach," she replied. And I'm like, "Speaker coach? OK." Again, at the time — it's crazy how God works — I was simply feeling the need to share my story to help inspire other people to live up to their potential. And there my friend was, telling me how good her speaker coach was.

I was like, "Wow, this is intriguing. Hey, I would love to have a conversation with someone like that." I never knew that particular service existed.

I requested a meeting with the coach, Dr. Kristen Guillory. I didn't know what to expect; I figured I'd be offered some tips or be urged to sign up for full coaching services.

But honestly, I was quite surprised. During a free session with Dr. Guillory, I told her about a speaking engagement I had at a school. I told her how I planned to start my speech — bid the class good morning and start talking about myself. Dr. Guillory told me, "Don't do that."

I had been preparing for this speech, or so I thought. But it was a true testament to people's craft. I'm an appraiser. You can't tell me anything about how to describe a house or how to determine and place a value on it. But it dawned on me that other people know their particular crafts just as well. Dr. Guillory went on to give me tips on how to deliver my talk differently and more effectively.

To get such instant feedback on something I was about to do was amazing. Being open to feedback is quite a thing when you're about to perform a task and you believe you're going to "kill it" — do it right. But this was something I'd never done before. I'd always been open to instruction and criticism from Phillip and other teachers/mentors — learning to appraise, learning how to buy a property, learning how to do mortgages. I have always been an open-minded person when it comes to learning something I don't know, period.

As a result of working with Dr. Guillory for just a short time and absorbing the steps and strategies she gave me, I got some of the best responses from that event at the school! One kid told me, "This was the best talk I've ever been to." That gave me the utmost confidence. Yes, I knew my amazing story. But to add a framework to it? That made it complete. Whether you're getting paid to do something like this or you're doing it for free, you want to be present and give your best.

I believe I was supposed to meet Dr. Guillory. She's such a gentle soul. She's big-hearted, spiritual, and just wants to see people do well. Honestly, I was very blessed to have crossed paths with her. Now that I've gotten connected to her, she's giving me the confidence to step into a crowd, do my thing, and go on to the next event.

Again, it's all just about being open. Don't think you know it all because you don't. Allow people to support you, people who know the particular area in which you could use support. You have to take your ego out of everything when you're trying to be successful at anything.

That's one thing about me. I've always absorbed other people's criticism. I take it not as an attack, but as them telling me, "Hey, here's some feedback. You can do what you want to do with it." I consider that a true gift because a lot of people get defensive when they're on the receiving end of feedback and therefore may not accept or use it. I've always received other professionals' feedback because I do that as an appraiser. When I put a value on a piece of property that isn't as high as a client thinks it should be for instance, I want that client to realize that although they think their property is worth X amount, the number I came up with is the actual value. So, I can't be a hypocrite. I can't expect an appraisal client to be open to my expert opinion but then refuse to be open to the advice I've sought from an expert in another field.

I repeat, I'm very blessed to have met Dr. Kristen Guillory.

Chapter 9

Becoming an Appraiser

Because the appraisal industry is one of the best aspects of real estate, it's the most overlooked part of real estate. Most people don't know until they go talk to a lender that appraisers even exist.

There are three different licenses involved in becoming an appraiser – state license, certified residential, and appraiser general. In appraising, if you're certified residential, you can do FHA (Federal Housing Administration) and VA (Veterans Administration) loan-related appraisals. If a homebuyer is obtaining a VA loan, they must use a VA-certified appraiser. It's the same with FHA — an appraiser must have a certain license to work with people who purchase homes with FHA loans.

Generally, you don't make as much money with a state license alone as you can after earning the second and third licenses. With a two-year college degree or a certain amount of college hours, you can actually skip the first license and go right to certified residential.

Speaking of college, let me back up and say that nowadays, you don't have to have a college degree to get that first license. Back when I got started, you had to be a college graduate to even begin training. Now, because the average age of the appraiser workforce is 51-65, it's understood that there will be more appraisers leaving the business in the next five to 10 years.

To get on the road to becoming an appraiser today you need only go to either the Appraisal Institute or McKissick.com, a platform by which you can take appraisal real-estate education and earn education hours. You can also Google your state and add the keywords "appraisal board," because each state has its own licensing requirements. If someone wanted to become an appraiser in Arkansas, all they'd have to do is Google "Arkansas state appraisal board" to see the Arkansas Appraiser Licensing and Certification Board qualifications.

Typically, there are about 79 hours of appraisal training, which include these courses:

- Basic appraisal principles (about 30 hours)

- Basic appraisal procedures (another 30 hours)

- A USPAP (Uniform Standards of Professional Appraisal Practice) class, which is a 15-hour course that involves appraiser comportment, i.e., information on how to conduct yourself as an appraiser

- A supervisor training course (about four hours)

After earning those education hours, a good way to find a mentor is to go to your state appraisal licensing board website and click on the roster. The roster will show you exactly how many appraisers are licensed in your state. (Here's a tip: It may be easier if you seek out a VA appraiser to work with. VA appraisers are a bit laxer than others when it comes to taking on apprentices; they'd be more willing to take you on because you can actually do part of the appraisal work.)

I'll emphasize here that if you are really serious about this business, you will want to take all your education courses, then cold-call or email some of the appraisers on that roster and say, "Hello, I want to become an appraiser. I've already completed my education hours." Why? Again, this business is complex. There's a lot to learn. If I were running an appraisal company, I'd probably only want to deal with someone who already had their education hours behind them, because sometimes people dip a toe into the industry, learn what's required of them, and find that it's not a good fit. That's the time a mentor/trainer will have wasted. So, start with the education requirements. Have all your coursework completed before you reach out to a licensed appraiser to see if they would be willing to take you on as a trainee.

A lot of appraiser education and appraiser knowledge in general. You can take the things you've learned and apply them anywhere. Today, I can value a property in a town without having ever been there. Appraisals in that town will follow the same general concept. Again, that's the beauty of the industry.

I'll add that there's definitely such a thing as continuing education in the industry, especially if you want to operate in another state. Although the basics are the same in all states, each state has licensing requirements that differ somewhat from the others. Some states have reciprocity with each other. Say you're licensed in Arkansas. If you want to be an appraiser in Texas, you can just fill out paperwork and send it in to transfer your license to Texas. But it could be different if you want to transfer your license from Arkansas to California. You may have to take additional tests, for instance. (Because I went from appraising in Arkansas to appraising nationally for a government agency, I never had to transfer my license anywhere.)

I've made previous references to the fact that my age and race put me in a tiny minority class of appraisers. The industry now recognizes that one of the issues this industry faces is its lack of diversity, especially when it comes to women, people of color, and young people. For a long time, no one would talk about this. That's changed because of another major issue the industry faces - a looming appraiser shortage. (The majority of appraisers in America are in the business for 20-30 years.)

This is why I've written this book — to highlight the appraisal industry; to say, "Hey, this is here. And it's so important to have more diversity in it."

What's sad, is that in Little Rock, I see even less diversity than there was when I began my career. To try to change this, I speak at colleges and at events I host. I'm trying to do all the things I know to inform people that this industry is wide open. In America, people will always want to know the value of their real estate assets. Nonetheless, it's not like this issue is at the forefront of real-estate topics. Most people think about the investor, the realtor, and the lender. They don't think about the "nerd" people, the people who are crunching numbers and compiling 30-page reports.

The job is worth going through the process, but people just don't know where to start. They don't realize that they can simply begin taking the courses online, something you can now do right out of high school. Obtain a trainee license through the state, find an appraisal company to apprentice with, then take the state exam to become fully licensed. Once you are a licensed appraiser, you can start your own company, working with banks and mortgage companies as well as appraisal management companies. Or you can sign on with a corporation that will pay you well to know how to put a value on a property.

I repeat here that you won't make as much money with the first license as you will when you get the second and third licenses, but it's a start. With that first license, you can instantly get a job and make what would probably be considered good money for a young person. After 2008, the vast majority of work came through the second license (certified residential) because you could do FHA loans, which most people get because they offer the lowest down payment. So that's probably the most popular license. But with a state license, you can still make decent money valuing properties. People still order market-value appraisals because they want to know their home's value before they sell. People still refinance. And you can charge probably $300-$400 per appraisal.

With the third license, appraiser general, comes the ability to appraise hospitals, airports, large apartment complexes, and big income-producing properties. Holders of the third license make two to three times more than holders of the second license because of the increased complexity of the job.

I can't say this enough — this is not an industry that you can get into and think you're not going to have to do some work. Earning a real estate agent license? Good. Fulfilling the requirements to become a mortgage lender? Great. But that appraisal license is going to be one of the toughest pieces of paper to obtain.

People see an appraiser come to a home and tour it for 20-30 minutes, taking measurements, taking photos, writing down the property's features and problems, and making say, $600 for doing so — and they think, "Dang, OK." But it's far more than that. The appraiser is taking all that data and putting it into a detailed report, after which he'll have to spend time figuring out the neighborhood's best home sales and comparing those homes to this property. True, appraisers do not spend that much time examining properties, and they are paid well, but they are doing more than people think. That's why appraisal training is so in-depth. You've got to really know your stuff because — yes, here I go once again — a financial institution is about to make a loan based on whatever you say about the property you appraised. You've got to know exactly what you're doing.

So, if you go after this career, you're going to have to have self-determination. You're going to have to sit down and tell yourself, "I see the light at the end of the tunnel. I'm going to do it. I'm going to put all my effort into it." This is definitely a career in which you're going to have to pull yourself up by your bootstraps and know that you're going to have to work through the process. If you do, it will pay off. Again, you are needed; When there is a mortgage loan involved people typically can't close a real estate transaction without you.

The most important reward of this job is the feeling of pride you get from knowing that you can objectively and accurately put a value on a property, the most profit-able price that it will sell for in a typical market.

PART TWO:
A REAL-ESTATE
PRIMER

Chapter 10

An Appraiser Weighs on the HGTV Shows

Among the most popular channels on your TV Channel lineup, these days is Home & Garden Television or HGTV.

HGTV specializes in shows in which tired, outdated, abandoned, and/or dilapidated homes are given a second lease on life thanks to the hosts/contractors/house flippers/designers who rehabilitate them. Here are some of the shows that have been featured on this channel: Love it or List It, Hometown, Good Bones, Fixer to Fabulous, Property Brothers, Forever Home, Fixer Upper: Welcome Home, And The former Flip or Flop. Most people in America are intrigued by how people do what they do in these shows, which I too find fascinating. I believe they offer amazing content.

The shows usually feature scenarios in which the hosts happily begin to fix up outdated or downright dilapidated houses, then find they must overcome challenges in the form of problems that materialize and threaten to eat up the previously set renovation budget. The element of surprise is strong, especially the ones in which people are buying and flipping homes. The flipper purchases a house and starts to do and/or supervise the work on it. Then the flipper is pulled aside by the general contractor, who says, "Termites have eaten up (whatever area)," or "The house has a foundation problem that will cost a fortune to fix." or "Um, look, they put an illegal addition on the back of the house that we have to remove; we don't have the square footage we thought we had."

Going beyond what is shown onscreen, however, I have to speak to those flippers that appear to be completely broadsided by issues that come up with the homes they're transforming. I doubt these flippers had no idea whatsoever of what they were getting into. In my opinion, all the homework (no pun intended) is done before the show. These people know many of the same things appraisers know. Of course, they know the home's "as is" value. Chances are they got an appraisal done on the house before production of that particular show episode began. We, appraisers, are not only going to reveal the value of the unrenovated property; we are going to estimate the cost of repairs and tell you what the property's as-repaired value is once it's fixed up. And, depending on the state you're in, you are required to pull permits for certain things you plan to do to the property you're fixing up.

What the shows correctly demonstrate is that with most rehabs, you're going to find some issue that was not apparent to the naked eye or with which you're not familiar. Take for instance, "Chinese drywall," something you will recognize only if you know and have been around properties that have been built with it. Wikipedia defines Chinese drywall as "an environmental health issue involving defective drywall manufactured in China, imported to the United States and used in residential construction between 2001 and 2009 — affecting an estimated 100,000 homes in more than 20 states." The drywall is said to have caused homeowners respiratory and other health problems. So, you may have to do more repairs if that's the type of drywall you're dealing with. But you can't "see" what you don't know about, and you don't know about what you can't see.

Look at the homes built in the 1950s, '60s, and '70s. Rehabbing wasn't as big of a deal then. They were doing it, but it wasn't an "appeal" kind of thing like it is now. Back then, people probably just wanted their homes to look nice, period. Now there are rehabbing trends. Homebuyers are saying, "OK, if the house doesn't have [a particular feature that's currently in style], I don't think I want it."

I believe the design trends have overtaken the industry because of the thought processes of redesigning properties. I mean, if you're looking at the '50s, '60s, and '70s homes, nine times out of ten you're probably going to want to take out a wall to create an open-concept space because of the trend. If you see the ceramic tile in the bathroom, you're going to want it gone, replaced with subway tile or some other tile that's big now. Ditto when it comes to dark paneling and sunken dens. As demonstrated time and time again on HGTV, popcorn ceilings are considered obsolete and unattractive. People don't want to see those anymore.

In my opinion, the hosts of these shows do a decent job of facilitating the trends and showing what people would like. The beauty of the shows comes in the creativity demonstrated. Homes can be updated with the addition of decks, patios (enclosed or uncovered), sunrooms, reading rooms, and mud rooms.

Traditionally, people have had interior decorators and designers come in and give a home a new look. Now, these home-interior professionals are part of the flipping process, creating residential masterpieces. And you want what your neighbor's got. You don't want to pay a certain price for a home if you don't have those buyer-centric things that are part of the latest trends - not only open-concept spaces but sleek, gleaming, all-white or nearly all-white kitchens (complete with farmhouse sinks!), spa bathrooms, specially textured fireplace frames, and his-and-her walk-in closets with built-ins.

Flippers understand that today's trends are what buyers like and want. And the HGTV flippers are showing how they can get a particular price for a home because of its appeal to a buyer. They're showing people what's hot in today's properties. Were these shows not around, a homebuyer might simply accept whatever a rehabber has done as long as it "looks nice." Instead, the homebuyer will say, "OK, I've got to have this, this, and this, because they're cool and everybody else I know has these features in their home." Home design has gone to the next level and HGTV pretty much demonstrates that.

Chapter 11

Real Estate Investing 101

There are different types of real estate investors. There are short-term investors and there are long-term investors. The short-termers — the ones who flip homes — buy-rehab-sell. Long-term investors typically invest in properties to take on a landlord role and rent them out.

I've enjoyed the best of both worlds. As a long-term investor, I have owned rental homes and Airbnbs in my career. One of my goals is to get into multifamily properties, i.e., apartment buildings.

In the world of short-term investing, I've learned much. When I was in Little Rock, I used banks for short-term investing. That's still a practical option today. But short-term investors these days are typically using other people's money to make money because real estate is a hot trend and most people who have money want to make money. Typically, if you can find the right "hard money" company or the right wealthy person to invest, you're in good shape. Everybody knows that value appreciation is a good thing in real estate.

If you ever want to consider making a real estate investment, I recommend using hard money lenders. They will lend money based on property, credit, and income. You will be given money to put down on a house flip or purchase a property that you can then rent out and earn residual income above and beyond the mortgage payment. Remember those lower-priced fixer-uppers I previously mentioned, homes that are in the not-so-prime neighborhoods? Those are really good deals. You can borrow money to purchase and fix one of those up and it can be your project (take your time). Once the home is fixed up, it's going to be worth far more than what you paid. You can use that equity, which is the difference between your mortgage payment and the home's worth, to buy another property or flip the house.

Finding Properties

When a property comes up for sale, the investor might say to themselves, "OK, this is an opportunity; do I want to move on it or not?" Typically, that's how investors pick up properties. Another way: They look to see what properties are going through probate — properties owned by people who have passed away. The heirs, who don't want to deal with those properties, often opt to sell them for cash.

If you want to own a property with the purpose of renting it out and making more than your monthly mortgage payment, know that owning a rental property will net you a huge tax benefit. As a homeowner, you'll have certain responsibilities, such as property taxes and insurance. These are things you can write off on the property at tax time, along with the cost of any repairs. (Note: Knowing the market rent for the area in which your rental property is located is important. A lot of people don't know that you can engage with a real estate agent who can help you obtain that information. You can lose money if you don't know the typical market rent for properties that share square footage and bed/bath count. I'll get further into market rent later.)

Something that I tell young people is that unless you're going to go buy your dream house, chances are your first property will be obtained with an FHA loan, for which as I've said, many people opt because it requires a smaller down payment. A piece of advice I give: If you're not in a rush to buy your dream house, buy a multifamily property first. Say that there's a four-unit multifamily property on the market, a property with one vacancy. You can buy the building with an FHA loan and move into the vacant unit yourself, while the other three occupied units help you qualify to get the home you want. So, boom, that's an immediate investment right there. Or if you have the option to live elsewhere and rent out all four units, do that. The income from your renters will help you all the way to the front door of your dream home!

This is something I advise single people and people who have never bought a property before to do. And that's pretty much what I did. The first property I bought, I never occupied myself because it wasn't the area I wanted to be in. I did want to be in a position to start the wealth pattern of generating multiple streams of income. I've always had the mindset to go this route because I saw older people doing it. And then I was right in the thick of things, being in real estate, learning about mortgages, and realizing, "OK. I'm making $300 more than what my mortgage is. That's another $300 a month in income, no matter what."

You can opt for a path on which you'll never have one income again because you're thinking differently. And that's why I wanted to learn all the behind-the-scenes aspects of real estate. I knew there were many facets of it. But learning about mortgages — in particular, buying yourself a home and simply making payments on that 30-year mortgage, compared to buying a property and renting it out for more than your monthly mortgage payment — is everything. It's a game-changer!

I found this out at a young age because as an appraiser, you learn the different approaches to value. First, there's a sales comparison approach, in which you take properties and compare them to other properties to figure out the value. Second, there's the income approach, in which you determine value based on the income the property is currently producing. Third, there's a cost approach, where you take land depreciation and improvements to figure out what a cost-new value would be.

In appraising, if you're going to use the income approach, you're going to find out the market rent in different areas. "Market rent" is the typical rent amount a property may bring in an area or neighborhood. As I've said, you can find out market rent in preparation to become a landlord.

And all you need to do to achieve this is have the purchasing power - to have a good income, a decent credit score, and this understanding: "OK. It's not my dream home, but this is a property that I want to rent out for money to take my family on vacation or do something else I otherwise wouldn't be able to afford." It's a mindset thing. The typical buyer thinks, "Oh, I don't want to get this property because I'm not going to be here forever. This is a big decision." Yes, it's a big decision. But most people nowadays don't stay in one place for 30 years anyway. What you will get accustomed to, if you can make additional money per month as a landlord, is having those tenants/extra income.

The big misconception is, "If I buy this property, I've got to figure out what I'm going to do with it." Do your homework! In real estate, it's all about calculated risks. These people doing HGTV shows wouldn't be doing them if they didn't have a clue about what things are worth - or will be. When it comes to investing in rental properties, your real estate professionals give you the information you need, such as the typical market rent in the area in which your prospective property is located. Then you can go to a mortgage lender who will tell you what you'll pay per month for the property. If the lender says your monthly payment will be $800 — principal, interest, taxes, and insurance included — and a real estate agent says, "You can lease this property out for $1,200 a month, easy" — Boom! Now it makes sense.

It's not rocket science. It's just learning things that make sense if you're going to get into investing. It's doing all your homework, learning all the lingo, and then starting to try to put those things together.

Where to invest in rental properties

Good investors do their homework. They're looking at rental properties, noting the condition of each, and seeing what rents are being charged. Of course, those properties that are most likely to make money are considered by investors to be the best investments.

When you purchase and renovate a rental property, you'll use the appraiser's knowledge to set rents according to whatever you paid for the property. Your appraiser will have done an income approach on a multifamily unit, compared it to a similar-style apartment complex in the same condition and quality, and noted the market rent. That probably gave you, the investor, the knowledge to say, "Let's buy this property and rehab it because we can get X amount of dollars based on properties with a similar design style."

Investors will do market research on an unrenovated unit. That's how they decide, "We can start charging this now because there are similar apartment complexes that are selling right now per month with these fixtures, with this lighting, and with these amenities." They are justified in raising the rent because of the new amenities they have added via renovations.

It's the same with new construction. Investors see a new construction project similar to the future property. They say, "Ah! There's already something similar and this is what they are renting those apartments out for per month. This is a good deal." An appraiser can tell all this by using the income approach. (If you're the developer/builder of the property, you can get a subject-to-appraisal; again, the property doesn't even have to exist yet! You can tell what it's going to be worth and what the market rent will be all because of the research an appraiser does before construction begins. An appraiser general will probably be the appraiser involved.)

So, investors aren't putting up apartment complexes or buying distressed properties and rehabbing them just because they "think" these properties will do well. The investors have already done their homework. And they've probably paid an appraiser to figure it out for them.

When you own a rental property that's close — especially within walking distance — to sources of food, entertainment, etc., that's when you can really boost your rental rate. You are offering accessibility to amenities for which people are often willing to pay top dollar. Dallas, for instance, has numerous little communities that combine residential properties with restaurants, bars, shops, and other desirable features. For the privilege of living in such communities, people pay higher housing prices, which they're willing to do on a quality-of-life principle: They can go where they want to go without having to drive.

Unrenovated properties in up-and-coming neighborhoods always represent a prime investment. If you own such a property, you can either renovate it or sell it for a good price; the neighborhood is morphing into a desirable location in which property values and rents will rise.

How can you find out that an area is "up-and-coming"? Go to your city's planning and zoning meetings. Every city has a planning and zoning department. Check to see when and where the meetings are held; attend (they're free) to find out which areas in the city are being considered for rezoning and what the city's plans are. These meetings occur fairly often.

I believe these meetings are a starting point for many developers. They attend them and find out what the city is up to and where. Then they seek land or a fixer-upper in an area of interest, helped along by full market studies that look at demand and capacity in the area. It's all market driven.

One example in Little Rock is the area where a Topgolf facility is planned, the Village at Brodie Creek in the western part of the city. Those who own properties in that area? Their property values, along with rents and home sales, are about to shoot up due to the arrival of that massive entertainment piece and the resulting influx of new people.

Capturing the interest of a would-be investor

Investors are capital-driven people. They've got to see something that is going to make a profit. So, one thing to do is start learning how to identify an asset. It's all about bringing a good deal to an investor. How do you know something is a good deal? You figure out what someone's trying to sell a property for, then compare that to what the repair costs would be and what you could sell the property for.

There's a typical 70% rule that most investors look at to see whether or not something is a good deal. According to this rule, explained at the website rocketmortgage.com, "real estate investors should pay no more than 70% of a property's after-repair value (ARV) minus the cost of the repairs necessary to renovate the home."

But knowing how to identify those properties means you're probably going to have a better chance at success with them than just taking on any old property that just needs to be repaired. Just because a property needs repairs doesn't mean you can say, "OK, this is a property I'm going to take on as an investor." No, you need to do your homework on this property, because the as-is value could be higher than what it should be. There's this big misconception in investing that just because a property needs repairs, it's a good deal. But you're going to overpay for a property that needs to be fixed up if you don't know the numbers. It's about knowing the numbers and knowing what investors like as far as ROR (rate of return) — trying to figure out the right ROR in order to make an investor pull the trigger. Showing that you know the numbers are more likely to get him to want to invest because you have done your homework and figured out what you need.

Before you buy, it's good to get a home inspection first to see what a property's roots and bones are. That's going to give a prospective contractor advance knowledge of what's actually wrong with the property; that contractor can then give you a repair estimate. Doing as much homework as you can is going to cause that investor to say, "Hey, I'm willing to invest in you because you've got a home inspection here. You know the bones of this property. You've got a contractor estimate here. Most importantly, you know from the repairs needed what we can sell it for, based on you doing your homework."

I think that is the big thing - knowing every facet of the deal. Now issues come up, so you always want to add a contingency percentage into your deals. But knowing the ins and outs — having everything lined up in a given timeframe, knowing the numbers, and showing a good ROR — will definitely help to capture investor interest. If you did your due diligence to go find a property that's a good deal, why wouldn't the investor help close on this deal? They wouldn't have found the deal without you.

Rental Property Maintenance

People tend to think, "OK, I've got to do all these things with this property." I think that's a big misconception. When I got into this, I didn't know what I was doing really. I just knew numbers. And I knew that real estate was a way to make money. Everything else, I just kind of learned along the way, especially property upkeep — the things you need to do regularly to keep up a home. Things such as:

■ Checking all the home systems before summer.

■ Doing all inspections of major components of the home to make sure no problems develop.

■ Preserving the property; for instance, if the property is a frame, throw a coat of paint on it every few years. Or if the property is brick and settlement issues pop up via cracks in that brick, addressing it immediately, rather than 10 years later when there's a big foundation problem.

I believe it's a mistake to simply harbor the attitude of "If I buy this property, I'll have a lot of responsibility." Yes, that property comes with a lot of responsibility. But can you "endure" having more money per month better than you would without actually having that property? The former is the better situation! You're going to be able to go to that ball game or whatever because you've got an extra few hundred dollars coming in.

Another thing: If you're going to own a rental property, you want to make sure you get additional insurance that covers your appliances - your heating, ventilation, and air conditioning (HVAC) units, etc. There are home warranty companies to which you can pay a premium each month; if anything covered in your policy breaks down, it's repaired or replaced at no additional charge. You can include part of the premium costs in the rent.

Chapter 12

Landlording 101

I purchased my first property for rental purposes. I had no intention of staying there. But because I had the appraisal knowledge, I knew it was a good deal based on the numbers the property gave me. Honestly, I bought the property sight unseen; because it was such a good deal, I had to make a quick decision.

I had an advantage here. (Again, appraisers know how to estimate repairs.) If the house was totally trashed and I had to redo everything, it was still going to be a good deal.

I came in as an investor and bought the property from the bank that held their note. This is common. Stuff happens - you never know what someone's going through - and properties go into pre-foreclosure status. Those are pretty much the best properties to buy because the owners, for whatever reason, are not able to afford the house.

But here's the thing: The property was still occupied by owners who had been about to lose it. At the time, I was in my mid-20s. The people who held the property were in their mid-40s. I had to go and introduce myself as the new owner.

It was a real intimidating situation. I'm thinking, "They're my parents' age and I've got to sit them down at the table and tell them, 'Hey, I'm the new owner. I don't know what your mortgage payment was but I intend to charge the market rent. If you want to continue to live here, this is what you'll have to pay, and we can do a contract."

It was crazy to me. I was scared, I won't lie. "Do I need to call somebody to go with me?", I wondered. That whole situation was just kind of hairy.

I didn't know what was going on with the couple, but I knew I probably saved them from foreclosure.

Anyway, I met them, and it turned out to be a really cool situation. I went and introduced myself as the new owner, brought them a rental contract, and we entered into an agreement. That was a happy ending.

Typically, you'll go looking for tenants for your property and in most cases, you have the privilege of vetting them first.

Seeking Tenants

When it comes to getting the word out that you're looking for tenants, the sky's the limit these days. I've never advertised properties online or via websites. I've always just used a local newspaper and word of mouth. I was listing properties for rent when social media wasn't really a big thing, so the local paper was everything to me.

Of course, advertising online/on a website is a major option today. You can also list your property with a listing agent. There are multiple listing services — real-estate broker-established databases exist that yield information about properties for sale; users can also find rental properties listed there. Putting signs in a neighborhood is an option; so is, contacting the area church and using other community resources such as businesses and hospitals. People at these institutions often know someone who's looking for housing.

Selecting/Dealing with Tenants

People need to know the ins and outs of renting properties before they get into landlording. I will say that doing background checks on prospective tenants — seeing what their pasts say about them — really helps. Not to judge anyone, but you're about to allow someone to inhabit property that you own - and that's business. You want to know whom you are letting into your property! Often a landlord will give a tenant the benefit of a doubt, and then it winds up biting the landlord in the butt.

So, when I meet a prospective tenant for the first time, I look at more than the rental application and the credit score. For instance, I'm probably going to walk by that person's car or ask for detailed information from their previous landlord.

Remember, these people are going to be inhabiting your properties, so you've got to look for clues. Definitely do a background check. Definitely verify that income, just to make sure everything adds up. And then have a conversation with your tenant hopefuls. Ask specific questions to find out a bit more about them.

When you're in a landlord role, you have to have tough skin. We as humans, like to attach emotion to things, but you have to ask yourself: "Is this business, or am I here to help people?" Sometimes, in the desire to help people, it can be all too easy to forget this is a business. I'm not arguing against showing compassion and grace to a tenant who occasionally gets in a tight spot. But this is a business arrangement. If you allow tenants to constantly give you sob stories (accompanied by an imaginary violin) as to why they can't pay all their rent, can't pay rent on time, or can't pay it at all, you're going to end up losing money by "helping people." As I've stated, you've really got to take your emotions out of it. At the end of the day, you have to decide whether or not you want your business to take precedence over being Mr. Nice Guy/Ms. Nice Gal.

Although this is about business, it doesn't hurt to build rapport with your prospective tenants. I think that's what a lot of people miss out on - the communication between tenant and landlord. Obviously, a tenant wants a nice place to rent. And you, as a landlord, want to make sure that you get your rent every month, don't get your property torn up, and don't find yourself facing a lot of other hairy issues you didn't foresee.

(Typically, owners hire property managers to deal with their tenants for them. The property manager is paid a percentage per month, something around 10% of rental income, to take care of such matters as background checks, moves in, moves out, repairs, etc. I myself have never had a property manager. I manage everything myself. I know the ins and outs of real estate and know what to do if issues come up.)

Check to make sure your would-be tenant will be a good fit in the neighborhood in which your property is located. If it's in a community populated by a lot of older people, for instance, try to find a tenant who lives quietly. You don't want the neighbors to say, "Oh, wow, I guess there's a new tenant over there because we're having to call the police every week." It's just a matter of being conscious of the neighbors. I believe residents of a neighborhood, especially longtime residents, appreciate that — landlords who won't rent to just anybody.

An Open Letter to Renters

Renting a property? That's fine. There are great benefits to renting a property. You know what your payment is per month. If you have a lease agreement, you know you have stewardship over this property for a certain amount of time. And with renting comes the flexibility to relocate fairly quickly. Once your lease is up, you can pick up and move to another property in your city of residence, in another city, another state, or another country.

However, I do feel the person who owns that property you're renting is the biggest beneficiary. Unless the property is paid off, you are literally paying the owner's mortgage and putting money in the owner's pocket every single month.

What most people do not know is that it's free to see whether you qualify for a mortgage. If you've had a job for two or more years and can produce two years of income tax returns, you can go to a mortgage lender and apply.

The lender will check your credit and tax returns, as well as your last two check stubs to verify your income. At any rate, it's simply good to see where you are credit-wise and see how much you can afford based on your current situation.

I suggest you start the mortgage application process before house shopping. (If you are found to be unready to take on a mortgage, start making changes to become ready. If you need to start working on your credit, for instance, view your credit report. Look at the things that are hindering you from having a high credit score. Pay those things off and dispute any incorrect negative information in order to improve your credit.)

Let's say the lender tells you, "All right, based on your current income, you qualify for a mortgage of $200,000." Again, for free, you can engage with a realtor to see what homes you can get for $200,000. This may motivate you all the more to purchase: "I can get this type of house? I didn't even know that!"

Unfortunately, all too many people are stuck where they are because they've become comfortable with where they are. They never want to look outside the box. They don't realize they probably could qualify for a nice house.

Based on what you're comfortable paying, you can look at what you've been doing for the past 12 months. That monthly payment you're making to a landlord? If you're comfortable with that payment amount, you need to stay around that amount when going through the mortgage process. Let's say you're approved for $200,000 but, based on what you're comfortable paying, you need to look for a house that's around $180,000. Staying with a home price you can afford puts you in a position to be prepared for any unexpected expenses — house-related or otherwise — that may come up.

One of the major advantages of home ownership is that you are able to gain equity, typically every year. I have a feeling that a lot of renters out there don't understand property equity. It's the real thing! Instead of renting — which benefits the person who owns that property — you could be benefiting yourself, even if it's just a modest dwelling that needs a little love. Here's what you're thinking should be: "This is my starter home. This property may need repairs, but I plan to stay here for five years and do repairs - one major repair every year. Then, in five or six years, I will have gained equity. I will have fixed the house up and can make a profit reselling it."

People also don't realize that they can actually buy a starter home by using down payment assistance programs. NACA (Neighborhood Assistance Corporation of America) offers a great program that gives you all the knowledge you need and helps take some of the fear out of home buying and homeownership. There are other such programs; most cities have them. Usually, you can talk to a local realtor, who should be able to tell you what's being offered in your area.

Bottom line: Owning property is one of the easiest ways to start wealth-building. Again, when you get that first property, establish a strategy to dwell there for five or so years, keeping in mind that home values appreciate based on where you bought your house. Then look toward selling and buying a bigger/better property. It's the easiest investment in America. You just have to have the purchasing power to do it.

I feel there would be more homeownership if people knew more about property equity and realized they didn't have to feel "tied" to the property just because they bought it. Even if they don't sell, they can always rent the property out.

Afraid of the process? It's all about simply seeing what the options are. You don't have to pull the trigger. But if you investigate and weigh your options — for free, with a loan originator — you might find you're more prepared to be a homeowner than you think you are. And you will be able to compare renting to owning. If you've got to make payments to have a roof over your head, you might as well be paying into something from which you can actually benefit.

This is valuable information for college students that don't know the differences between homeownership and renting. (These are some of the things I talk about when I speak at colleges.) They also have no idea whom to engage with in the real estate process, period. A tip on finding a realtor: When you're engaging with a realtor, you want to know that they're actively engaged with you because you will typically be dealing with them for 20 to 30 days. You want to make this experience optimal. Communication is everything. You want to be with a realtor who's knowledgeable about every aspect of the process. Seek out someone you feel comfortable with. If you don't get a good realtor, you may have a bad first-time home-buying experience and be reluctant to go through it again.

Chapter 13

Reading an Appraisal 101

Most people who experience an appraisal as first-time homebuyers don't know how to read the report. They don't know what the appraiser is doing at the property. In many cases the realtor doesn't know much about the process either, having gotten only a little bit of information about it in real estate school. Let me take you through the appraisal process.

When someone requests an appraisal, the appraiser's job is to identify what's going on with the house. Earlier I mentioned the various reasons for appraisals, from a purchase or refinance to someone simply wanting to know the market value of their property.

Let's say it's a purchase. The appraiser will receive the order. The appraiser will call the realtor or the property owner to set up an inspection. Note to sellers: Before enlisting the services of an appraiser, it's imperative to do one's own property inspection — check for any problems with the roof or the foundation, check for any house-settling problems, check for termites, etc.

Examining the property

When the appraiser goes to the property, the first thing he or she will do is introduce himself to the homeowner, agent, or whoever's there, if anyone. Using a measuring tape or laser measure, the appraiser will go around the house collecting all of the outside walls' measurements to figure out the square footage. While the appraiser measures the property, he's going to look around and make sure nothing needs to be repaired.

(What most people don't realize is that not all of a property is considered part of the square footage, only the above grade heated and cooled areas. A garage, for instance, is not included in square footage.)

The appraiser will note all he sees. Again, he's vastly different from the home inspector. The home inspector will go through that property thoroughly to find anything that may be wrong with it. The appraiser is only going to write down what he or she sees from the naked eye.

After he completes the exterior inspection, the appraiser will go inside and note such things as the kind of heating source being used, the type of flooring surface (hardwood, vinyl, carpet), and the types of appliances found in the home. He will note the condition of the kitchen and bath(s).

Then he'll give the property a condition rating - poor, average, or excellent. Typically, properties are in average condition unless they've been remodeled.

If the appraiser sees something that needs to be addressed/repaired, he will make a note of it. (If the property has some type of foundation or settlement issue on the exterior walls, the appraiser may note that a construction engineer, or someone qualified to do foundational work, is needed to do the repairs.) If a lender sees that the appraiser requires the issue(s) to be fixed before signing off on the property value, that problem, no matter what will have to be fixed before the lender distributes any funds. (Home inspections come with no such requirement.)

Inspection of the property is just part of the appraisal process. Taking all that data and putting a report together is how the appraiser determines the final value of the property. In compiling this report, the appraiser will find comps. Other homes that have sold within the neighborhood and that compare to the property will be used for comparison. Generally, in appraising, apples must be compared to apples, but it's not always the case. For instance, you may have a three-bedroom property you're appraising, but when you look at the comps in the area, you find that one of the best sales is a two-bedroom house. So, adjustments must be made to get back to "apples to apples." In comparing the property to be appraised, the value is what is referred to as "adjusted" value. The appraiser is going to figure out all the differences between the comps and the subject and after everything's adjusted, come up with a value range. He will set the final value within that range.

Sometimes people will say, "But I needed my property to be valued at $160,000. It came in at $150,000." Well, that's because $150,000 was the opinion of the appraiser and within the adjusted gross range. So, it was warranted.

Anatomy Of An Appraisal Report

Page One of the appraisal report consists mostly of the appraiser's data collection results, customarily public information taken from county records. (You can go to the county website and research any property; put in the address and you'll get a map reference, the subdivision where the property is located, and other information. This information is entered into the appraisal report.

The appraiser notes those properties on the market that compare to your property and includes them in the report, along with the many exterior and interior photos they took during the appraisal process. The report will reflect things that have occurred at the property, as well as how the appraiser arrived at its value, in the addendum section.

The first two lines on Page Two show the number of listings and the comps in the neighborhood. Then it shows a range of sales in the neighborhood. So, you can look at your appraisal value and make sure that value is within the range of sales the appraiser lists on the property. That's a good thing to know. (Many people, once they get the appraisal, simply go to Page Two, look at the value, and that's it. I show people how to look beyond that for such things as whether there are similar homes for sale and whether they're within a mile of the appraised property.)

Also on the appraisal report, the appraiser will indicate whether the property is in a flood zone. That's how people know they have to obtain additional insurance for the property. In Florida, for instance, people will probably have to have flood insurance because of how often it floods in parts of Florida.

Again, the appraiser is there for the buyer. Most sellers think their property is worth more than it actually is, or they just want a certain amount of money for it. Its true value can be checked only by someone who is trained to determine that value. So, the appraiser is an investigator but he's trying to protect you as a buyer. The appraiser is there for the lender too because a bank doesn't want to lend any more than it should for a property. Just because a seller wants $200,000 for a house doesn't mean it's worth $200,000. It's worth the value an appraiser says it is.

So, appraisers keep sellers honest, protect the buyer (if you buy a house whose value was said to be far more than what it's really worth, you can be underwater on your mortgage on Day One), and help lenders calculate their risk. The lender needs to know they're giving you this money to buy this thing, and it needs to be worth at least what someone is trying to sell it for or more. If it's worth less, you will have to renegotiate the contract. You're going to have to figure out whether the seller wants to come down to where the appraised value is. A seller wanting $300,000 for a house that's only worth $280,000? That's a huge problem. You should not purchase a home unless an appraiser says it's worth what the seller is trying to sell it for or more.

An appraiser is also good for people who want to flip houses; they know they can engage an appraiser to figure out what a property is worth when it's repaired. That's important because a flipper is going to buy the property at one price, repair it, and sell it for another price. If you're the flipper, you've got to know how much it's going to cost to repair the home, but then you've also got to know how much to sell it for. If you know those numbers, you will know whether this is a good property in which to invest. The appraiser is the person who knows all that information and can give you an estimate to help you understand whether you're getting a good deal. With multifamily properties, it's the same thing; an appraiser's report will include an estimate of what the property will bring in rental income and what its value would be based on the production of that income.

A couple of tips if you have to get a home appraisal for selling purposes:

■ Always keep the path clear to walk around your home to make way for the appraiser to measure the property. You want to make it easy for him to do his work.

■ You definitely want to share with the appraiser the things you have done to upgrade the property — for instance, the repairs you have done — and place a dollar amount on those upgrades. That can sway the appraiser's opinion in your favor. They are human after all; they may miss something. If you give them a list of what you actually did, they probably will take it into consideration in setting value.

■ As a matter of fact, before you engage an appraiser, complete all planned renovations because the appraiser will give an "as is" value on the day of the appraisal. If the appraiser goes to your property and sees you've got half the flooring pulled up, he may have to note that! And your property may not be valued for as much as it would have been.

Chapter 14

An Open Letter to Future Real Estate Appraisers and Valuation Analysts

If you are considering a career in the appraisal industry, let me emphasize (again) that it's a one-of-a-kind industry. The mere concept of participating in the most pivotal part of the home-buying process is extremely important. The funny thing is, you have to hear about this career from a family member or friend - or when you buy a home, and your mortgage professional tells you an appraisal is needed before you close on your home loan. And typically, people who get into this industry have already worked another job for many years or may have retired and wanted to get into a more self-schedule-controlled career.

Thank goodness this is currently changing. More people are learning about this wonderful industry. One of the best things about this profession is that you get on-site training with a mentor to learn everything you need to be successful.

I have a friend who is much older than I am and recently got his license. His life changed from night today. So did mine! I was able to not only work for myself but travel the world and live comfortably in my mid-to-late 20s. All because I decided to take this industry seriously and learn what I needed to know as an appraiser.

Starting out, you will need to have the mindset and determination not to stop until you get that license, no matter what your state's requirements are to earn it. It's easy to get distracted because, as I've indicated earlier, there's a lot you have to learn. It's not an easy task to go through the courses and be taught by a mentor. But at the end of the day, it's going to be worth it.

Most consumers who get a home loan in America are required to get an appraisal before they close on the home. So, this industry is not going anywhere; people are always going to need someone to know how to value real estate. Although I easily obtained a mentor through knowing him growing up in church, the onus was solely on me to learn and develop the mindset needed.

Outside of the education and licensing requirements, I would like to give you some points to consider helping you be as successful as I have been in this career:

■ From the start, I was very curious. Wanting to know and learn about real estate and real-estate terminology was a benefit for me.

■ In this profession, logic, and reasoning is huge. Everything really just has to make sense. (For example, when appraising a property on the coast, there may be comparable sales that have an ocean view selling for around $500,000. If the property you are appraising does not have the ocean view, it may not be worth as much.)

■ Being flexible is everything in this profession! Your mentor may need you to do multiple things, things outside a regular appraisal report. For me, it was filing papers and taking pictures of properties. You must keep a level head and take the time to learn all the things you need to know.

■ Ethics is key as well. In this profession, you must maintain a high level of public trust in your assignments. Just know that the values that you are placing in any given market will be comparable for someone else looking to refinance or sell in that same area; if your numbers are off, it could adversely affect another person's deal. So be ethical - even when it's inconvenient. Be completely objective and without bias on every appraisal assignment. Provide a fair estimate of the market value for the property. Accurately identify and help stakeholders understand a property's characteristics or red flags. Be confident and competent on every assignment.

One of the more technical duties of being in the appraisal industry is making sure you know how to identify the problem, which is the first rule in appraising. Knowing who the client is and labeling the effective date is extremely important. If you ever have to go to litigation, the first question they could ask is: Did you identify the problem?

■ Knowing how to collect data is especially important. On every appraisal you are tasked with doing an interior/exterior inspection of the property, so you have to know the ins and outs of home terminology and how to label conditions accurately.

■ Next, there is analyzing data! Understanding the property's marketability, i.e., evaluating supply and demand locally and nationally, is huge. Knowing how to determine the subject's highest and best use is also important.

■ Thirdly, you need to know how to apply the different approaches to value. In the industry, there are approaches appraisers use to value different property types. The first is the sales comparison approach; this is the most common appraisers use. They compare the subject property to other properties that are comparable in quality, size, and location. Next is the cost approach, where appraisers are charged with determining the cost to replace or reproduce a property. And last is the income approach, in which the appraiser comes up with the value using the net operating income the property brings in.

The beauty of the appraisal industry is that it allows you to quickly and easily enter into entrepreneurship. You can also gain the expertise needed to value property by becoming a valuation analyst for companies that deal in real estate. In my case, I was able to start an appraisal company at 26 years old. There's a lot to learn in running this type of business, but it is doable; you definitely want to know that you are ready and able to not only do the appraisal work correctly but be able to handle conversations when challenged about a value or the inner workings of your appraisal report by the lender. It's OK to continue to work under a mentor or get a job that could use your expertise until you are ready to strike out on your own.

Chapter 15

An Open Letter to a First-Time Homebuyer

Homeownership can seem like a scary process and it's a huge responsibility. But it's worth it in my opinion.

True, timing is everything when it comes to owning a home. Short-term housing may be what someone needs at a certain point in life because it's the most convenient. But "convenient" is a term that sometimes causes people to settle for less than what they could have. I believe that when situations and circumstances are too "convenient," they keep us from growing in life. To grow, we must stay motivated and know our worth.

What I have learned from being a homeowner is that the risk can be highly beneficial. Most people think they are going to be stuck with the house if they take on this type of investment. People buy and sell properties every day, hour after hour, so that's a myth.

Another myth about homeownership is that owning is more expensive than renting. Typically, a mortgage can cost less per month than what's needed to rent. The most common mortgage uses an amortization schedule of 30 years, but most people upgrade, or downgrade properties depending on their lifestyle and never really pay on that mortgage all 30 years. Not only do you get to have private space as a homeowner, but if you choose to live in another state or buy an additional home, you can use that first asset to make money by putting the property on the rental market or making it an Airbnb in your area. Potentially you could make an extra few hundred bucks a month. Not only can you add to your monthly income; you can take advantage of home appreciation. (This occurs when your home or investment property increases in value over the years of owning the property.) So, owning a home has major benefits: You can make money when you sell it or obtain rental income.

When people buy and sell property that is in close proximity to yours, those properties might well bring in higher prices than what you paid, which helps increase your property equity. Meanwhile, you can easily see what your equity is by getting the property appraised or consulting with a local realtor. Property equity can help send your kids to college or you can pull money out of your house to make other investments, as opposed to just renting and giving landlords/investors your money. You don't have to buy the biggest property on the block. You can simply opt for an affordable, non-upgraded starter home; you can even buy a property that needs repairs. In my opinion, this is the most doable option. You can figure out where you are financially and what you can comfortably pay per month. You can, for free, go check with a mortgage lender to figure out what you qualify for.

Life is all about strategy. Find the property that fits your amount, whether or not that property needs repairs. These days, they even offer additional loan programs to refurbish homes. But, if you don't want to take on additional debt, you can take advantage of your low mortgage payment and simply take your time repairing the property, which is only going to help increase its value.

Utilizing this idea of getting a starter home and rehabbing it yourself will potentially allow you to have enough equity to put down on your dream home. Renting is great if you plan to live in an area only temporarily, but in my opinion, you are throwing your money away every month. Homeownership is always the best option, whether the interest rates are higher or lower at the time.

If you have children: Consider the experience to be a learning process for them as well. Imagine gaining knowledge of real estate with the added benefit of it helping your kids. One suggested scenario: After you buy your first home, start saving money for a down payment to buy a property in the city of your child's chosen college or university, a place where that child can live instead of paying room and board as part of the college cost. You'll be setting your child up for their first investment! You could find, say, a three-bedroom property that needs repairs and fixing it up. Move your child into the house when he or she enrolls in college. The other bedrooms can be rented out and potentially pay the mortgage and generate additional money you can give your child. After four or five years, the property will, ideally, have gained equity after graduation. You can give that income-producing property to your child to set him up. He can continue to rent the property and already have investment income along with a paycheck.

Real estate is how people supplement their income. No matter where you live, housing is a necessity and with homeownership, you can benefit from rental income and property equity.

Chapter 16

A Letter to My Younger Self

Marcus,

You cannot imagine what's about to happen in your life! I know things are getting a little hectic for you in middle school, but just continue to be your own person, and don't follow the crowd.

I realize it's crazy for you to see Centennial Park, the place at which you played with friends, featured on an HBO documentary called "Gang War: Bangin' in Little Rock," which highlights the crime and gang activity in the city. But try to stop worrying about all the negative things you see every day, and please continue to ignore the opportunities to sell drugs or be in a gang. You will grow up to live a life of always doing the right thing, even when no one is looking.

I'm proud of you for being so strong mentally when most people you know in the neighborhood are getting in a lot of trouble. I know you really appreciate going to Grandma's house every morning to get breakfast before getting on the school bus. Hug Grandma and Grandpa a little tighter each day.

Be grateful for the wonderful connection with your family, especially your grandpa. He will become your best friend over the years. Continue to soak up all the times you get to follow him around the church, watch a sports game, or just talk about life with him.

By the way, one of his greatest joys will be to wake up at his home in 2022, open the newspaper and see you featured on the cover of the High-Profile section of Arkansas' only major, statewide daily newspaper. You will both have a moment reading the story in which you are referred to as a "double unicorn" because of the things you have accomplished in your life.

Thank you so much for setting the goal as a middle schooler to graduate from college. The goal of graduating from college, along with learning how to live a life of discipline, and wanting to represent your family well, will benefit you in more ways than you know. There will be some tough moments but continue to be strong and ask for help. Continue to lean into all positive friendships from school and church. They will keep you motivated.

Sir, you will not believe what happens to you after achieving your goal of college graduation. You will find your passion for learning multiple areas of real estate and things will take off quickly. It will be like a breath of fresh air for you.

I want you to know that all the traumatic experiences you are going through now will be displayed as an adult in words like Drive, Passion, and Achievement. After you learn about real estate appraising, you'll be motivated to start your own company in a field in which the average age in the U.S. is 50 years old, but you will join that field and become CEO of an appraisal business at the age of 26, just two years after graduating from college. Because of your accomplishments, you have been able to travel to many places and live a comfortable life at a young age. And you will get an opportunity to learn about the whole real estate industry by participating in appraisals, mortgages, and investments.

Your discipline and goal-oriented mindset will pay off as you get a once-in-a-lifetime opportunity to work with Fannie Mae, a leading source of mortgage financing in the United States and be there for over a decade and become one of the youngest African Americans in the country to put values on residential properties in every state in America. God has his hands on your life the entire time, and He brings all the right people into your life to help you. Then, you get to share your story of beating the odds and share your real estate knowledge with youth and adults in many states. You also get to be a mentor in the first-ever Appraiser Diversity Initiative with Fannie Mae and the

Appraisal Institute. Every time you talk with a mentee you will inspire them to go through the journey of becoming an appraiser. Your passion for appraisals and real estate will be felt by every mentee you help. You will impact multiple people in different parts of the US. At this point, you have had the courage to write a book and give all the knowledge you have learned over the years about real estate and appraisals to the world. Mom always taught us to help one another and to be of service first.

Thank you for taking the hard path of being different and applying discipline and integrity to everything you do. Know that you never let anything or anyone come between you and the life you always dreamed of.

Sincerely,

Marcus

TESTIMONIALS

Kacy Parham, Certified Residential Appraiser

To my dear friend and fraternity brother Marcus Hill, two words describe you: determined and motivated. Determined to achieve despite the world surrounding you and motivated to push through adversity and change when challenged. Hence, inspired me to push through a long and rocky road to achieving my appraisal license and creating my own appraisal company (Affordable Appraisal Services).

To your readers: My conversations with my brother concerning the appraisal industry, or just catching up with him, sharpened the iron. I encourage you to flip through the pages of this book and allow his story and wisdom to sharpen you.

Jennifer Ballheimer, Regional Production Manager, Mortgage Financial Services

I met Marcus and started working with him in 2005. Marcus brings his years of experience and dedication to his job and has aided hundreds of families as a loan originator. He is one of the most driven and compassionate people I know, with a great depth of knowledge and a desire to help and educate all those around him. Marcus has a keen eye for finding efficient and honest solutions to any problem.

His level of perseverance never fails to impress, and his consistent willingness to go the extra mile has been evident throughout his entire career. It has been my sincere pleasure to witness Marcus' growth and watch him impact the lives of so many people around him.

Jamal Bonds, Senior Loan Officer, Bank of England

I, Jamal Bonds, and my co-worker at the time, Paul Wilkins, met Marcus Hill back in 2007 at our place of work, Bank of England Mortgage in Little Rock, Arkansas. We were fortunate enough to have the chance to work with Marcus, a young Black appraiser looking to build relationships with local bankers such as Paul and me. We gave him his first contact order for an appraisal, and he did a great job in a timely fashion.

I came to know that I could count on Marcus for a timely appraisal and could be certain that the market value given by him had been carefully researched and heavily scrutinized. His character, work ethic, and loyalty are through the roof. He is thorough, precise, considerate, accurate, aware, professional and, to top it off, easy to work with. I was constantly impressed by his work and determination to provide us with great service.

Tommy Branch, Little Rock, Arkansas Homeowner

Back in the early 2000s, I bought my first house. I had no clue what was needed; I certainly didn't know I had to get an appraisal. I asked my realtor at the time whom I should call, and she recommended Mr. Hill. From the beginning, Mr. Hill spared no details in telling me what was wrong and what was right with the house. He also treated me like family from the start. He was kind, beyond professional, and right to the point on everything. For that, I was very grateful and felt blessed to have him in my corner. Anyone who is around him will know that he really cares about helping people reach their goals and their potential, wherever they may be in life.

I'm very thankful that Mr. Hill was someone I could count on.

Roderick Pittman, Mentee and future Appraiser

Since Marcus began mentoring me as an up-and-coming appraiser, my view of the industry has expanded beyond assessing the value of assets. He has challenged me to assess my own worth and encourages me to bring my whole self into the profession. Each time we speak, he has been an open book, nurturing me through his wealth of experiences coupled with the humility of a servant! I am filled with gratitude for the path that he has paved.

ACKNOWLEDGMENTS

First and foremost, I want to thank GOD for putting the real estate appraisal industry into my life at such a young age. I want to thank him for the ambition, passion, and driven mindset that has stayed with me over the years. Without His wisdom, I would not have had the drive to learn the hardest profession in real estate, and therefore, would not have written this book.

I want to thank my family, especially my mother and grandpa, who taught me to have a kind heart and help others and be of service first.

Life is beautiful when you can meet and surround yourself with people who inspire you and help you grow. A special thank you to Phillip Thompson of Little Rock, Arkansas. Thank you for introducing the world of real estate to me right out of graduating college. You allowed me to find my passion and I am forever grateful. Without your desire to get into the appraisal industry, I would not have had the opportunity to learn this great career.

To all the real estate appraisers and real estate professionals I have met over the years who have aided me in some way, I want to say thank you for your patience and willingness to support me.

A big thank you to my colleagues at Fannie Mae. Thank you for taking a chance on me even though I was a very young appraiser when hired. At the time of this book's release, I am one of the few to have placed a value on thousands of residential properties in every state in America - all because of this wonderful opportunity.

I want to thank all the mortgage companies, banks, real estate agents, and consumers in the city of Little Rock, AR. Thank you for looking past my age and giving me the chance to help in the closing process of your real estate transactions. Because of you, I had the opportunity to give my opinion on the value of thousands of residential properties in the city.

I also want to thank all my friends, childhood church members, my brothers of Kappa Alpha Psi Fraternity Inc., and speaker coach Dr. Kristen Guillory, who pushed me to be the best version of myself. Thank you for the motivation and encouragement, as this book would not exist without each of you.

A special thank you to my editor, Helaine R. Williams of Make it Plain Ministries. You were a GODsend and I appreciate everything you have done for me.

ABOUT THE AUTHOR

Author Marcus Hill is a real estate trailblazer whose diverse portfolio spans from real estate appraisal and property management to loan origination and real estate investments. At 24 years old, his career in the real estate industry was sparked when he was introduced to the appraisal process.

Hill began building the foundation for his success. Almost a decade later, he continues to be an industry leader and one of the youngest to have placed values on residential properties across the US through a Fortune 100 company.

Hill continues to use his knowledge and expertise as a dynamic speaker to the youth at high schools, colleges, non-profits, community organizations, and conferences. He also organizes home buying, credit building, home loan, and appraisal workshops in neighborhoods where real estate and appraisal information is scarce. Hill's true passion is to inspire future generations to find careers in the real estate appraisal industry.

WEBSITES FEATURING

MARCUS HILL

https://www.urbanartsonline.com/home/marcushill

https://www.youtube.com/watch?v=1wtFJAl4BEU

https://www.arkan-sasonline.com/news/2022/sep/04/marcus-hill-escaped-a-rough-childhood-and-found-a/

https://www.linkedin.com/in/marcus-hill-b08546b8/

https://www.heartandsoul.com/education/busi-ness/valuing-the-american-dream-marcus-hill/

https://shoutoutdfw.com/meet-marcus-hill-real-es-tate-and-appraisal-expert/

BIBLIOGRAPHY

"Chinese Drywall." Wikipedia, Wikimedia Foundation, 13 Nov. 2022, https://en.wikipedia.org/wiki/Chinese_drywall.

Field, Anne. "What Caused the Great Recession? Understanding the Key Factors That Led to One of the Worst Economic Downturns in US History." Business Insider, Business Insider, https://www.businessinsider.com/personal-finance/what-caused-the-great-recession.

Rafter, Dan. "What Is the 70% Rule in House Flipping?" What Is The 70% Rule In House Flipping? | Rocket Mortgage, Rocket Mortgage, 30 Dec. 2022, https://www.rocketmortgage.com/learn/what-is-70-rule-in-house-flipping.

"U.S. Valuation Profession Fact Sheet Q1 2019." Appraisal Institute, https://www.appraisalinstitute.org/file.aspx?DocumentId=2342.

"What Is the Dodd-Frank Act?" Findlaw, 21 June 2016, https://www.findlaw.com/consumer/securities-law/what-is-the-dodd-fran
act.html#:~:text=The%20DoddFrank%20Act%2C%20also%20known%20as%20the%20Dodd-Frank,Federal%20Reserve%20under%20the%20Troubled%20Asset%20Relief%20Program

www.ingramcontent.com/pod-product-compliance
Lightning Source LLC
Chambersburg PA
CBHW051635120626
46551CB00014B/2090